Cambridge Elements

Elements in Forensic Linguistics
edited by
Tim Grant
Aston University
Tammy Gales
Hofstra University

ONLINE CHILD SEXUAL GROOMING DISCOURSE

Nuria Lorenzo-Dus
Swansea University
Craig Evans
Swansea University
Ruth Mullineux-Morgan
Swansea University

Shaftesbury Road, Cambridge CB2 8EA, United Kingdom

One Liberty Plaza, 20th Floor, New York, NY 10006, USA

477 Williamstown Road, Port Melbourne, VIC 3207, Australia

314–321, 3rd Floor, Plot 3, Splendor Forum, Jasola District Centre, New Delhi – 110025, India

103 Penang Road, #05–06/07, Visioncrest Commercial, Singapore 238467

Cambridge University Press is part of Cambridge University Press & Assessment, a department of the University of Cambridge.

We share the University's mission to contribute to society through the pursuit of education, learning and research at the highest international levels of excellence.

www.cambridge.org
Information on this title: www.cambridge.org/9781009314640

DOI: 10.1017/9781009314626

First published 2023

A catalogue record for this publication is available from the British Library.

ISBN 978-1-009-31464-0 Paperback
ISSN 2634-7334 (online)
ISSN 2634-7326 (print)

Online Child Sexual Grooming Discourse

Elements in Forensic Linguistics

DOI: 10.1017/9781009314626
First published online: September 2023

Nuria Lorenzo-Dus
Swansea University

Craig Evans
Swansea University

Ruth Mullineux-Morgan
Swansea University

Author for correspondence: Nuria Lorenzo-Dus, n.lorenzo-dus@swansea.ac.uk

Abstract: This Element examines technology-assisted grooming of children for sex – henceforth, online grooming – as an illegal practice of communicative manipulation and, as such, something that research within the academic field of forensic linguistics is ideally placed to help counter. The analysis draws upon online grooming datasets of different sizes and provenance, including from law enforcement, and deploys different analytic techniques from primarily discourse analysis. Three features of online grooming discourse are focussed on: groomers' use of manipulation tactics; groomers' abuse of power asymmetries; and children's communication during online grooming. The Element also discusses ways in which findings derived from richly contextualised analysis of online grooming discourse can – when combined with co-creation projects involving child-safeguarding groups, children and lived-experience experts – add considerable value to societal efforts to counter online grooming and other forms of online child sexual exploitation and abuse.

Keywords: online child sexual exploitation and abuse, grooming, manipulation, discourse analysis, corpus linguistics

ISBNs: 9781009314640 (PB), 9781009314626 (OC)
ISSNs: 2634-7334 (online), 2634-7326 (print)

Contents

Series Preface

The Elements in Forensic Linguistics series from Cambridge University Press publishes across four main topic areas: (1) investigative and forensic text analysis; (2) the study of spoken linguistic practices in legal contexts; (3) the linguistic analysis of written legal texts; (4) explorations of the origins, development and scope of the field in various countries and regions. *Online Child Sexual Grooming Discourse* by Nuria Lorenzo-Dus, Craig Evans and Ruth Mullineux-Morgan is clearly situated in investigative and forensic text analysis and shows the power that a corpus linguistic approach brings to the detailed description of a specific area of criminal activity.

Nuria Lorenzo-Dus, Craig Evans and Ruth Mullineux-Morgan are all intimately part of Project DRAGON-S, funded by the Safe Online Initiative at End Violence against Children, which brings an applied focus to their work through the production of software tools based in the insights from their language analysis. This analysis firmly identifies grooming as goal-driven communication and they demonstrate how the offenders achieve their goals through the operation of a variety of powerful stances and manipulations. They also show how, on some occasions, a child attempts resistance to these coercive practices. They go on to consider the roles the child might play in these interactions and how the representations of the child can reduce their perceived and actual agency.

Overall, this Element provides a thorough and important exploration of this difficult area of research and makes a powerful contribution to tackling a significant social problem. It makes a valuable contribution to the growing linguistic literature on online sexual offending and should be read not only by linguists with interests in the area, but also by psychologists, criminologists and those from other related disciplines.

Tim Grant
Series Editor

1 Introduction: Contextualising Online Grooming

1.1 Aims

Online grooming is a digital practice by which an adult seeks to engage a child in sexually abusive encounters or relationships. As an illegal and immoral activity, it is a social problem, and one that research shows is growing due to offenders becoming more sophisticated in their use of grooming tactics and online interactions increasingly becoming the norm for children, among other factors (see Section 1.2). With this Element, our aim is to add value to existing efforts to tackle this social problem by focussing on language use, which is a central component of online grooming and has received scant attention to date (see Section 1.3). Language, broadly understood to include words and other semiotic modes, is the primary means by which groomers manipulate and control children online (Lorenzo-Dus et al., 2020). Therefore, to understand the practice of online grooming it is necessary to understand how groomers use language to engage in the practice of manipulating and coercing (thus, grooming) children. Also, given that online grooming is an interactional process (Lorenzo-Dus, 2023), a focus on how children use language in the context of grooming interactions is equally important. The linguistics knowledge that we share in this Element (Sections 3–5 especially) represents only part of how we seek to address the problem of online grooming. In addition, we provide an account of a research project, Project DRAGON-S, through which this knowledge can be applied to support frontline child-safeguarding practitioners (Section 6).

1.2 Rationale

Online grooming represents a major social problem across the world, one that has become more widespread as people increasingly lead their lives online. The boundaries between the so-called online and offline realms are blurred – online and offline spaces are inextricably interconnected and they intersect online and offline experiences (see, e.g., Jones, 2004; Androutsopoulos, 2014; Bolander and Locher, 2020; Lorenzo-Dus, 2023). It is the norm for personal and, increasingly, romantic relationships to be forged and maintained online, especially across a variety of social media platforms and benefiting from myriad digital affordances of smartphone, live streaming and burgeoning metaverse and gaming technologies. This is the social wallpaper against which children and young people are experiencing their formative stage of life – a stage where they are predisposed to seek out and develop meaningful social connections. The need to conduct personal relationships online increased during the global COVID-19 pandemic, with governments imposing restrictions on movement and meetings between people; for example, the lockdown measures introduced by the UK government in 2020 and 2021.[1] With children spending more time online, and often with the goal to develop new relationships, their exposure and vulnerability to adults targeting them for sexual abuse and exploitation has increased.

The scale of the problem of online grooming is suggested by a 2022 report published by Thorn,[2] a technology non-profit organisation dedicated to defending children from online child sexual exploitation and abuse (OCSEA).

[1] www.instituteforgovernment.org.uk/data-visualisation/timeline-coronavirus-lockdowns
[2] https://info.thorn.org/hubfs/Research/2022_Online_Grooming_Report.pdf

This report reveals that 40 per cent of children have experienced cold solicitation for nudes online. The same percentage of children (increasing to 47 per cent for female teens) report having been approached online by someone they thought was attempting to befriend and manipulate them. This echoes growing recognition that online grooming represents a form of 'cyber gender-based violence' that manifests wider challenges of marginalisation, violence and oppression, reflecting a cultural landscape characterised by significant gender disparities (Reynold and Ringrose, 2011; Ringrose et al., 2012). As a growing body of literature shows, teenage girls and LGBTQ+ youth are most at risk.[3] The Thorn (2022) report also finds that approximately a quarter of 9–12-year-olds see flirting with or dating adults online as common. In an earlier report in 2020,[4] Thorn noted the increasing trend of groomers to exploit the normalisation of online communication with strangers in children's lives, such as by using a 'scattergun approach' of contacting a high number of children to increase the chances of getting a response and gaining access to at least one child when they accept a chat or friend request.

The cause of the problem of online grooming lies entirely with the individuals who seek to sexually abuse and exploit children. However, online grooming as a social problem is exacerbated by a number of factors that support groomers' purposes while creating barriers to solutions to help improve the safety of children online. For example, definitional confusion in legislation relating to child sexual exploitation and abuse (CSEA) has created an impediment to addressing the problem of online grooming. Ongoing debates have their foundations in the historically shifting parameters of understanding surrounding issues of CSEA. Melrose (2013a, p. 156) describes this situation as discourse in flux, arguing that the 'refashioning' of language from 'abuse through prostitution' to 'sexual exploitation' has created a long shadow of confusion that continues to impact and shape practitioners' responses. A further source of exacerbation is the lack of regulation online. A 2019 report by the UK-based charity National Society for the Prevention of Cruelty to Children (NSPCC) highlighted the limitations of self-regulation among big tech companies, noting that 'voluntary codes … lack precise rules and standards, usually lack effective monitoring and oversight

[3] See, for example, www.coe.int/en/web/cyberviolence/cyberviolence-against-women; www.iwf.org.uk/news-media/news/campaign-launches-as-new-report-finds-girls-at-worsening-risk-of-grooming-from-sexual-predators-online/; https://info.thorn.org/hubfs/Research/Responding%20to%20Online%20Threats_2021-Full-Report.pdf; www.iwf.org.uk/about-us/our-campaigns/talk-and-gurls-out-loud-self-generated-child-sexual-abuse-prevention-campaign/; www.nspcc.org.uk/about-us/news-opinion/2022/online-grooming-crimes-rise/; www.nspcc.org.uk/about-us/news-opinion/2021/online-grooming-crimes-girls/; www.weprotect.org/wp-content/uploads/Global-Threat-Assessment-2021.pdf

[4] www.thorn.org/blog/online-grooming-what-it-is-how-it-happens-and-how-to-defend-children/

mechanisms, have weak (if any) enforcement mechanisms, and consistently do not impose any sanctions on sites that don't comply' (2019, p. 7).[5] Concern has also been expressed in relation to the rapid expansion of end-to-end encryption (E2EE) on instant messaging platforms, which threatens to intensify the harms that children can be exposed to online (NSPCC, 2021).

While the factors that exacerbate the problem of online grooming still persist, there have been changes that create prospects for an improved situation. For example, in the UK in 2017 a new offence of sending a sexual communication to a child came into force.[6] Further, the visibility that this new offence brought to the issue of online grooming through improved recording of cases means that the centre of perceived responsibility of keeping children safe online has started to shift. At the time of writing, the UK Online Safety Bill's[7] proposed regulatory regime and the European Union's (EU's) ambitious planned legislative package[8] represent forthcoming advances attempting to regulate the online space and enhance protections for children. Australia has also made legislative changes to how it regulates the Internet.[9] However, legislating to improve regulation represents one part of the whole system approach required to successfully tackle online grooming. Other parts/aspects will be considered in Section 1.3, where we look at how applied research, including our own, Project DRAGON-S, can support efforts to improve the safety of children online.

1.3 Towards an Applied Research Approach to the Language of Online Grooming

Applied research carried out to address the social problem of OCSEA in general, and online grooming in particular, has tended to have one of two primary objectives: detection or prevention. Detection has often entailed the development and use of methods from computer science research for the

[5] www.nspcc.org.uk/globalassets/documents/news/taming-the-wild-west-web-regulate-social-networks.pdf

[6] Following a successful campaign from the NSPCC leading to an amendment of the UK Serious Crime Act 2016: www.nspcc.org.uk/globalassets/documents/policy/nspcc-flaw-law-campaign-house-of-commons-serious-crime-bill-second-reading.pdf

[7] The UK Online Safety Bill would impose duties on 'regulated services' in relation to three types of content: (1) illegal content; (2) content that is harmful to children; and (3) content that is legal but harmful to adults. All regulated services would be required to protect users from illegal content and there are proposed additional duties for services accessed by children.

[8] The EU regulation would set out the responsibilities of relevant online service providers, requiring them to detect and report child sexual abuse online and to report it to public authorities. The EU Commission also proposes a European Centre to prevent and counter child sexual abuse. https://ec.europa.eu/info/law/better-regulation/have-your-say/initiatives/12726-Fighting-child-sexual-abuse-detection-removal-and-reporting-of-illegal-content-online_en

[9] www.abc.net.au/news/science/2022-09-21/internet-online-safety-act-industry-codes/101456902

purpose of identifying child sexual abuse material (CSAM) (see, e.g., Lee et al., 2020; Project Arachnid[10]) and other manifestations of OCSEA, including online grooming (see, e.g., Pendar, 2007; Kontostahis et al., 2009; Milon-Flores and Cordeiro, 2022). These studies typically integrate some form of language-based analysis, usually deploying natural language processing alongside sentiment, content or topic modelling analysis.

As for (O)CSEA prevention-oriented research, multiple foci have been pursued, ranging from awareness raising through to developing both holistic frameworks for protecting children, such as the WePROTECT Global Alliance's Model National Response (MNR) framework,[11] and educational programmes. Unlike in other areas relating to the prevention of violence against children, a comprehensive 2022 report by the World Health Organization (WHO) highlights an important gap in the evaluation of programmes aimed at preventing OCSEA.[12] This is significant, the WHO report further argues, given that the evaluation-based evidence in those other areas generally shows that such programmes are successful. In terms of OCSEA educational programmes that have been subject to evaluation (e.g., Chibnall et al., 2006; Davidson et al., 2009; Mikton and Butchart, 2009; Topping and Barron, 2009; Mishna et al., 2011; Walsh et al., 2018), the focus tends to be on the impacts on and improvements of children's knowledge of online safety strategies, digital dangers and high-risk online behaviour (UNICEF, 2020). The impact of such programmes on children's disclosures and the ensuing incidence of OCSEA has been rarely evaluated or examined (Lalor and McElvaney, 2010).

A notable limitation of much research into OCSEA, whether driven by a detection and/or prevention focus, is the failure to recognise some manifestations thereof, notably online grooming, as a communication-based practice. By not providing knowledge and understanding about the interpersonal dynamics at play in online grooming, for example, previous education programmes have lacked key information about how children can put e-safety advice into practice. This is not to say that a communication focus has been entirely absent from applied research in this area. For example, forensic linguistics methods were used in Pilgrim, a course run from 2010 to 2017 to train specialist police officers in the UK on how to convincingly simulate children's use of language during interactions with suspected groomers (see Grant and Macleod, 2016, 2020). Using a robust evaluation methodology, Grant and McLeod (2020, pp. 112–13) were able to demonstrate that 'linguistic identity assumption is challenging but can be trained'. However, this training served a specific operational purpose of law enforcement, while in training

[10] www.projectarachnid.ca/en/ [11] www.weprotect.org/model-national-response/
[12] www.who.int/publications/i/item/9789240062061

aimed at practitioners, caregivers and children more generally, very little attention has been given to the role communication plays in online grooming.

The ongoing work of Project DRAGON-S (of which all three authors are members) seeks to address the gap in linguistics research being applied more broadly to support practitioners in tackling the social problem of online grooming. Project DRAGON-S is an applied research project based at Swansea University, in collaboration with researchers at University of Toulon, that in 2021–2 developed two tools to be used by child-safeguarding practitioners. These are DRAGON-Spotter, a tool for detecting online grooming content that has been designed for use by law enforcement, and DRAGON-Shield, a training portal for child-safeguarding practitioners that focusses on online grooming as a manipulative communication practice. Project DRAGON-S mainstreams linguistics, synergising linguistic analysis and deep learning models in artificial intelligence in the development of DRAGON-Spotter, and linguistics and criminology, psychology and public policy research-based evidence, in the development of DRAGON-Shield. These tools have been developed in partnership (through consultation and testing) with practitioners, internationally and across agencies. In 2023 both tools are undergoing rigorous evaluation across the UK, Australia and New Zealand. The linguistics findings presented in this Element underpin the development of the Project DRAGON-S tools, in particular DRAGON-Shield. More discussion of Project DRAGON-S (its tools and applied research ethos) is provided in Section 6.

1.4 Note on Terms

In our work, we use the term 'groomer' to refer to an adult in the datasets being examined who is known to have committed the offence of sexual communication with a child in an online context. In some cases, the adult may have been convicted of other CSEA offences, which is why we sometimes use the broader terms 'offender' and 'perpetrator'. We use the term 'child', often as part of the compound 'child-target', to refer to an individual aged 0–18. The WHO (2023) defines childhood as a period between the ages of nought and nine and adolescence as the period between the ages of ten and nineteen. Yet, under UK legislation (the Serious Crime Act 2016), the offence of sexual communication with a child applies to children under sixteen, unless the contact is from a known adult in a position of trust – in these instances the age range is extended to anyone under the age of eighteen. We recognise that in child-safeguarding practice the term 'children and young people' is often preferred to differentiate between younger and older children. However, in the analysis presented here we use 'child' (and 'child-target') as an umbrella term.

Further information about our terminological choices is provided in Section 5. In that section, we discuss the implications of word choice with respect to victim-blaming language, and our rationale for using certain words to represent child communicative behaviour.

1.5 Structure

This Element is divided into three parts. The first part (this section and Section 2) sets the scene. It explains our understanding of online grooming as communicative manipulation and explains the novel and necessary contribution that such an understanding can make to crime prevention and detection efforts. Data and analytic methods are also described in this part, as well as ethical and researcher well-being aspects of direct relevance to the study of OCSEA. The second part consists of three sections (Sections 3, 4 and 5), each of which is themed on a feature of online grooming discourse, namely groomer tactics and performativity, groomer power abuse and child communication. The analyses in these sections deploy different analytic methods, which are introduced in those sections for reader convenience, including how they support the particular research questions being addressed in each section. The third part comprises one section (Section 6) – a conclusion section that also reflects on the ways that the linguistics research presented in this Element can be applied to practice to help address the social problem of online grooming. This is in part illustrated via Project DRAGON-S.

2 Online Grooming As Manipulation Discourse: Concept and Method

2.1 Introduction

> The power to manipulate beliefs is the only thing that counts.
>
> Michael Ende (1979), *The Neverending Story*

The quote above, from Ende's novel, corresponds to advice that a dying werewolf, named Gmork, gives a boy warrior, named Atreyu, who has been charged with saving the magical kingdom of Fantastica. He must do this by finding a human, a boy named Bastian, who must give the kingdom's empress, a female child, a new name. Time is of the essence and Atreyu must find a way to 'manipulate' a child (Bastian) to achieve the goal of saving Fantastica quickly.

There is something compelling about the power of manipulation attested by the literary and media success of Ende's (1979) novel – Gmork's continuing advice shows deep fascination with the control that can be achieved by manipulating others: 'Who knows what use they'll make of you? Maybe you'll help them to persuade people to buy things they don't need, or hate things they know nothing about, or hold beliefs that make them easy to handle, or doubt the truths that might save them.'

In this Element we define online grooming as a practice of communicative manipulation, specifically as an adult's use of technology-mediated communication comprising multiple modes to get a child to partake in sexual activities online and at times also offline (Lorenzo-Dus et al., 2016, 2020). Although the examples of the ends of manipulation given by Gmork pre-date the Internet, they resonate. We see how technology not only mediates but also facilitates manipulation: groomers' manipulation may result in children turning away from – possibly hating – others in their support networks. The manipulation may also lead children to believe that having sex with an adult is normal, which may increase their likelihood of acceptance to perform sexual acts online with and/or for their groomer. It may lead to their wrongly believing, once they are sexually involved with their groomer and realise that they are being abused, that it is their fault. This can trigger feelings of shame and self-blame, creating a barrier to disclose the abuse to others who may be able to help them.

Each of these scenarios – and others examined in this Element – are the by-product of sophisticated manipulative communication in online grooming. This section provides the theoretical and methodological underpinnings to enable such examination. Section 2.2 offers a brief overview of the concept of manipulation, calling for linguistic approaches to move away from traditional analyses that seek to identify 'manipulative language features' (e.g., specific deictic forms, use of negation, etc.) and towards analysis of manipulation discourse in context. This enables characterisation of online grooming as a *sui generis* practice of communicative manipulation (see Lorenzo-Dus, 2023). Section 2.3 shifts attention to the empirical analysis of online grooming as manipulation, specifically to our methodology. Herein, we subvert academic genre conventions of firstly introducing one's dataset and, next, the procedure and analytic frameworks deployed, including research ethics and integrity considerations. Instead, given the relatively unexplored issue of research on distressing data, we foreground the latter, with a focus on researcher well-being (Section 2.3.1). Sections 2.3.2 to 2.3.5 describe our data and methods.

2.2 Conceptualising Online Grooming As Communicative Manipulation

Manipulation has been extensively examined across several disciplines, ranging from philosophy and rhetoric studies through to politics and linguistics. Much of this work has also sought to define manipulation vis-à-vis related concepts such as influence, argumentation and, most frequently, persuasion. The main difference between persuasion and manipulation – most scholars agree – lies in the notion of consent, which the former has and the latter lacks (O'Keefe, 2006; Nettel and Roque, 2012). Yet, as Pardo (2001) explains, the ability to consent is linked to power relations between persuader/manipulator and their target(s), which may in turn depend on factors such as the institutional space in which their discourse happens, their respective authority roles and so forth.

Van Dijk (2017, p. 206) argues that (social) manipulation is 'a form of domination or power abuse [that] involves organizations or institutions as manipulating agents making use of power resources, such as access to or control over knowledge or public discourse'. Van Dijk (2017) further argues that those being targeted for manipulation tend to have fewer resources, for example knowledge, which makes it particularly hard for them to resist such domination. As Section 4 will show, this is the case in online grooming, in which the adult–child relationship is set within wider patriarchal power structures that necessarily entail a marked knowledge differential and hence power imbalance, both skewed in favour of the grooming adult.

Another difference between manipulation and persuasion concerns their respective spheres of impact. Here there is no academic consensus, however. For example, Sorlin (2017) argues that, unlike persuasion, manipulation goes beyond changing mental states and into the actional level. Yet for Van Dijk (2017, p. 206), 'mind control' is the primary aim of manipulation, 'action control' being an indirect, secondary aim.

A further oft-cited difference relates to morality. Persuasion, Partington and Taylor (2018, p. 3), for instance, note, 'is of itself neither good nor bad, neither beneficial nor harmful'. This is not the case for manipulation, the philosophical study of which has been largely predicated on the premise that manipulation is harmful (see, e.g., Bakir et al., 2019 for an overview). As noted earlier, linguistic approaches highlight the potential, indeed likely, negative effects of textual manipulation, be that in terms of cognitive (Van Dijk, 2006, 2017) or actional (Sorlin, 2017) control. However, the focus of the linguistic analysis remains anchored in its discursive features.

Numerous discursive features have been identified as being regularly deployed in manipulation discourse. For example, Van Dijk (2017, pp. 207–8) provides the following examples of manipulation structures and strategies:

- grammatical sentence structures
- biased (e.g., derogatory) lexical items: implications/implicatures, generalisations
- forms of actor descriptions

- granularity and other modes of situation or event description: more or less precise or complete, detailed or vague, close versus distant and so on
- storytelling
- argumentation
- superstructural (schematic) categories, such as headlines in news reports
- general ideological polarisation between in-groups (Us) and out-groups (Them).

Similarly, considerable work has been devoted to identifying the linguistic markers of deception, which is itself seen to be a common manifestation of manipulation. This research has tended to use natural language processing and/or psycholinguistic profiling software, such as Linguistic Inquiry and Word Count (LIWC; Pennebaker et al., 2015). The LIWC list of linguistic markers of deception includes the use of vague language and negative textual forms (Bachenko et al., 2008; Addawood et al., 2019); the use of 'words that can be used to exaggerate – subjectives, superlatives, and modal adverbs'; and larger percentages of interrogative words (how, what, when), third-person plural pronouns, question marks and terms such as 'true' and 'truth' than in non-deception contexts (Davis and Sinnreich, 2020).

However, as Lorenzo-Dus (2023, p. 47) argues, 'reliance on largely decontextualised, computational approaches presents some limitations – not least because of the lack of one-to-one mapping between form and function in language use'. These features 'are neither manipulative/deceptive per se nor manipulation/deception signalling across communicative contexts. They provide a valuable repository of knowledge, in as much as the strategies are seen to work in specific research-evidenced contexts' (2023, p. 47). Lorenzo-Dus (2023) thus calls for a context-rich, identity-foregrounded approach to the study of manipulation overall and online grooming as a *sui generis* manifestation thereof.

Regarding context, it is paramount to see online grooming as digitally mediated manipulation. Its digitalness, as it were, reflects and shapes its features, and it relates to three key areas: sharing, trust and engagement/influence (Lorenzo-Dus, 2023). Online grooming 'exploits the digital sharing era in which we are said to live, specifically the positive cultural rhetoric about sharing concrete (e.g., pictures, files) and abstract (e.g., advice, opinions, personal experiences) objects online' (2023, p. 195). Groomers regularly engage in self-disclosing talk via which they share feelings of vulnerability, such as loneliness and fear, thus contributing to building trust (Lorenzo-Dus, 2023). Online grooming requires the grooming adult to be able to gain access to and then continuously engage – or seek further contact with – the child being targeted online, with that engagement possibly extending to the offline realm too (see Section 3). Such engagement varies in part depending on different affordances within and across digital platforms. As noted in Section 1, groomers may start with a scattergun approach, contacting the child on a given digital platform, and then move to a higher-privacy/encryption platform to try to satisfy particular abusive goals.

As for identity, Lorenzo-Dus (2023, p. 203) argues that groomers' manipulative discourse is premised on attempts at 'identity homogenization', whereby they seek to

> construct themselves and their targets as inhabiting a perfectly aligned ideological, affective, and overall identity space. The better aligned they are, the more likely it is that they will see themselves as being misaligned from other equally homogeneously constructed identities: their opponents . . . The alignments being sought all entail transgression of legal systems and/or moral orders.

It is in relation to these legal systems and/or moral orders that one may see online grooming as a *sui generis* form of manipulation. 'The illegality and/or immorality of online child sexual abuse and exploitation . . . are far from mere secondary considerations in relation to the kind of manipulation practices that characterize [it] . . . the stakes of getting things wrong, as it were, are very high in terms of social and/or legal sanction' (Lorenzo-Dus, 2023, p. 203). As Section 3 will show, this shapes groomers' discourse, for example in terms of seeking secrecy as part of their tactical communication.

There are, of course, some commonalities with manipulation features overall. These features include covertness, power asymmetry, coercion, intentionality (goal driven), speaker (i.e., manipulator) interest prioritisation and insincerity/deception (Lorenzo-Dus, 2023). Covertness, power imbalance and intentionality are regularly used by groomers. At a global (or macro) level, covertness features across all online grooming – 'the illegality and/or immorality of the behaviors involved making this a *sine qua non* therein' (2023, p. 198). Intentionality is also always present – groomers' discourse is goal driven. As will be detailed in Section 4, power asymmetry is brought along by the broader context of online grooming, including the fact that it entails communication between an (often male) adult and an (often female) child. But groomers also bring power asymmetry about during interaction with the children that they prey on.

As for speaker interest prioritisation, this is also salient in online grooming. Given the illegality and/or immorality of the behaviours being pursued, the targets' interests cannot be aligned to those of the groomers. This, as Lorenzo-Dus (2023, p. 198) explains, does not mean that groomers 'always present their work in zero-sum game terms ("by going along with my intentions, I'll benefit, and you'll lose"). Instead, and as part of their covertness work, [they] strive to present full alignment between their own and their targets' interests'. This often means investing in 'other-stance attribution' (Coupland and Coupland, 2009), whereby the groomers attribute the stance of 'keen learning about sex with adults' to the children they target. Such a stance 'is presented not just as being compatible with the groomers' stance of sexual expertise but also as being a natural activity for the target, as something that all minors engage in' (Lorenzo-Dus, 2023, p. 198).

Explicit coercion, in the form of threats and harassment, features in online grooming interactions. Its impact on the child can be particularly negative given the inherent power asymmetry of the adult–minor (and highly gendered) relationship in which coercive discourse is deployed. As will be seen in Sections 3–5, moreover, 'coercion tends to be sugar-coated through facework that relies on positive and negative politeness strategies' (Lorenzo-Dus, 2023, p. 199). As for insincerity/deception, this is not always present in online grooming as far as the manipulator's identity is concerned. Some (as opposed to all) groomers lie about their age, gender, marital status and so forth, and this can be deduced from their online grooming interaction in some cases. In contrast, determining deception about their goals (e.g., are their references to love and friendship (partly) genuine?) is not possible using linguistic analysis techniques only.

2.3 Analysing Online Grooming Communication

2.3.1 Researcher Well-Being

The analysis of online grooming chat-log data is likely – or at least perceived at some point – to be distressing for the researchers concerned. After all, grooming and other types of CSEA are generally seen as one of the most abhorrent forms of criminality and moral deviance. 'At some point' and 'perceived' are deliberate word choices. Dictionary definitions of the term 'distressing' refer to something that causes extreme sorrow, anxiety or pain.[13] So, we are operating within the realm of emotions and, hence, subjectivity. Some topics are, if not inherently distressing, certainly 'primed for' triggering distress – for example, terminal illnesses or deviant and criminal behaviour (such as online grooming). However, it is important to acknowledge that topics can become distressing for some researchers, and not others, in certain contexts, but not others, and at particular points in the research journey. The sensitive and distressing nature of research can not only become apparent during data collection – as has traditionally transfixed ethics committees – but

[13] See, for example, the *Oxford English Dictionary* (https://languages.oup.com/research/oxford-english-dictionary/).

also during data analysis and dissemination. As researchers, we may also find distress arising unexpectedly in our participants, or in ourselves. So, 'distressing data for whom, when/where and why?' may be better questions with which to approach this issue.

Academic researchers of distressing content are exposed to risks of vicarious trauma, and there is evidence of it developing in some cases (e.g., Woodby et al., 2011). This is more widely recognised, and therefore better supported, in disciplines such as psychology and criminology than in others like linguistics. There is a real dearth of research on the impact of distressing textual content on language scholars (but see Lorenzo-Dus, 2021). Perhaps this is because of the assumption that linguists 'just' deal with texts and words, which are presumed to provide a distance from the humans that authored them, and therefore a shield for the language analysts. Yet, the analysis of language – especially of language in context – can be a fully immersive experience. As Section 3 will argue, moreover, in relation to the application of Austin's (1962) and Searle's (1969/1975, 1978) theories to online grooming, language is action – rather than just words.

The case for the (linguistics) researcher's well-being needs to be clearly made. What is more, the onus on such well-being cannot be solely placed on the researcher. Self-care is crucial. But there is a need for institutional enablement of self-care. This means institutional buy-in, financial and otherwise, for developing and monitoring implementation of support measures, such as flexible working arrangements, built-in de-compression leave, pleasant workspaces and access to mentoring and well-being counselling. And it means embedding these measures across research projects, from application stage (if relevant) through to post-delivery stage, and certainly throughout the many stages in between. One key stage is seeking and securing ethics approval where, in addition to data-oriented aspects (privacy, security, etc.), researcher-oriented considerations need to encompass both integrity and well-being, for example limiting as far as possible exposure to distressing data. There is also an important leadership role for funding bodies in reviewing how to make systemic changes to address and improve researcher well-being. Echoing debates about child safety online, for as long as the onus is on individual institutions and students 'to keep themselves safe' within wider environments that are not fit for purpose, the impacts of dealing with distressing data will not be adequately recognised, understood or addressed.

Ethical approval for research for this project was secured at the outset from Swansea University. Certain aspects of the broader project within which it was generated required additional ethical approval. A case in point was the Lived Experience Expert Project, which is discussed in Section 6.

2.3.2 The Data

The analysis in this Element is primarily based on chat logs containing online conversations between groomers and the children they have targeted. They represent interactions across a variety of social media platforms (e.g., Skype, Facebook, WhatsApp, Kik) where groomers typically access children via their publicly viewable profile information (bio and photo), and where contact is initiated by selecting requests to connect options built into the platforms. This dataset, hereon referred to as the Law Enforcement (LE) corpus, is the one used throughout this Element (unless otherwise stated). It consists of approximately eighty online grooming chat logs from the period 2014 to 2019. These were purposively sampled from a larger dataset of online child sexual offending (approximately half a million words) to account for socio-demographic variables of groomers and children. This dataset was secured as part of a UK law enforcement data-sharing agreement for research purposes.[14]

Another dataset discussed in this Element consists of over 600 chat logs (c. 3.3 million words), from the period 2004 to 2016, and collected from the website Perverted-Justice.com. This dataset, hereon referred to as the Perverted Justice (PJ) corpus, contains conversations between groomers and trained adults pretending to be children (decoys). Owing to it being publicly available and challenges with accessing authentic groomer–child interaction data, chat logs from the PJ website have tended to be used in most of the research on online grooming, including in studies of online groomer discourse (e.g., Chiang and Grant, 2017; Lorenzo-Dus et al., 2020).

While similarities have been identified between groomer discourse in the PJ and LE corpus, as will be discussed in Section 3, questions have been raised about the reliability of online grooming data involving decoys. Chiang and Grant (2019, p. 693) argue that this 'undermines the continued use of PJ data as good proxy data for research into genuine online CSA [child sexual abuse] conversations' (2019, p. 693). Additionally, reliance on decoy data has meant that the discourse and thus voices of children have been rarely addressed in previous research. Our focus on the LE corpus in this Element reflects the importance we assign to the analysis of groomer–child interactional dynamics.

A further dataset that is used in the research presented in this Element is PAN2012. This is a 21-million-word corpus consisting of online chat from adult dating websites, online grooming and technical chat (for a detailed overview see Inches and Crestani, 2012). In our research we have used PAN2012 as a reference corpus when processing the LE dataset using corpus linguistics

[14] The agreement precludes further details about the dataset being provided here.

methods (see Section 2.3.5). Having identified and discussed the data used, we next summarise how it was prepared for analysis.

The data used to create the LE corpus was provided unredacted. Therefore, the first data pre-processing undertaken by the research team was data anonymisation. This entailed manually replacing all personal identifiers (names, locations, IP addresses, telephone numbers, etc.) with generic descriptions, such as [child's first name], [school name] and so forth. The resulting dataset was further processed using the spelling standardisation software VARD 2.5.4. The purpose of standardising spelling is to support the use of corpus linguistics approaches (see Section 2.3.5), which use software to identify linguistic patterns that spelling variation might otherwise cause to be missed. The LE corpus was then uploaded to the web-based corpus processing system CQPweb (Hardie, 2012), in readiness for being analysed using several corpus linguistics procedures built into the software. The LE corpus was also uploaded to NVivo 12, a software package that supports data annotation and qualitative analysis. The other datasets used in our research, the PJ corpus and PAN2012, were downloaded from their respective websites, the spelling standardisation process using VARD was applied to the PJ corpus and both datasets were uploaded to CQPweb.

2.3.3 Discourse Analysis

In this Element, discourse analysis broadly refers to the process of identifying, describing and explaining features of language use in texts and investigating patterns of these features across texts that belong to the same type of language use situation. By 'text', we mean any language-based event with an identifiable beginning and end, and which has a material form to make systematic analysis possible. The texts examined in this Element are chat logs: digital texts that constitute the record of conversations between groomers and child-targets via different social media platforms. By 'features of language use', we mean their form (e.g., a word or word type) and their function; that is, how they create both lexico-grammatical meaning and social actions. This reflects our understanding of discourse as 'the pragmatic process of meaning negotiation' (Widdowson, 2004), where language is not only used to convey information and express ideas but also has a relational dimension: what Halliday (1994) refers to as the interpersonal meta-function.

To understand the social function of language used in texts, it is necessary to consider closely the context in which the texts occur. For this reason, context is a key concept in the study of discourse, and a number of models of context have been proposed by linguists (see, e.g., Hymes, 1974; Halliday, 1978; Van Dijk, 2008). These models identify specific situational or cognitive factors to be methodically considered when analysing texts, though some have been criticised for being restrictive and including categories that are open to interpretation (Jones, 2012). The approach we take in this Element is to not use any particular model of context but to include in our analysis a consideration of contextual factors that are relevant to the study of online grooming and that emerge as salient in the course of examining the data. Aspects of context we pay particular attention to include the knowledge and attitudes of participants (e.g., groomers' and children's goals; children's approval-seeking, attitudes to risk, etc.); discourse type (norms and practices associated with manipulation discourse in general and online grooming discourse in particular); and communicative space (i.e., that it is online and remote).

Understanding the context in which a particular text has been produced may determine the features an analyst chooses to focus on. For example, they might examine evidence of persuasive strategies in a text with no overt persuasion because they know it is an advertising text that has the purpose of getting people to buy a product. The selection of features and how these are interpreted can also depend on the particular theoretical framework used to analyse the use of language. In discourse analysis, there are a number of widely used frameworks for analysing how people use language to relate to each other. These include (im)politeness theory (e.g., Brown and Levinson, 1978/1987; Culpeper, 2011), which focusses on how language is used to manage positive and negative face needs and avoid face-threatening acts, and speech act theory (Austin, 1962; Searle, 1969/1975, 1978), which views utterances in terms of the social actions they perform. These frameworks have previously been used in research on online grooming discourse (Lorenzo-Dus et al., 2016; Lorenzo-Dus and Izura, 2017; Lorenzo-Dus, 2023). They are also used in this Element and are discussed in more detail in Section 3.

Other frameworks focus on the structure of texts, for example genre analysis (Swales, 1990). This involves identifying 'discoursal or rhetorical units', known as moves, which each serve a distinct pragmatic function in a scheme that constitutes the text type of a particular genre (Swales, 2004, p. 228). Moves were identified in a study on online grooming discourse that highlighted the 'broad structures' of grooming interactions, though, owing to the variation between conversations, these moves were not found to fit a specific scheme that could be said to represent a grooming genre (Chiang and Grant, 2017, p. 103).

A researcher's approach to analysing discourse is also sometimes based on their interest in a particular subject or theme, which may determine the linguistic or textual features they select for examination. For example, if a researcher is interested in how identity is discursively constructed, as has been the subject of some notable works (e.g., Benwell and Stokoe, 2006; de Fina et al., 2006), there are certain features that naturally lend themselves to studying this, such as pronoun use, naming terms, narrative and so on. Even though it is not always necessary to use particular theoretical frameworks when analysing discourse and identity, these do exist (e.g., social actor representation; see, e.g., van Leeuwen, 1996). Discursive identity has been the focus studies of OCSEA that draw on a variety of theories to investigate ways in which identity is created for grooming purposes, for example (Grant and Macleod, 2020; Lorenzo-Dus, 2023). Another subject that has frequently been a focus in discourse research is power, which we discuss in Section 4.

As has been shown in this section, the process of choosing what features to focus on when analysing discourse will often be influenced by pre-existing factors; that is, a researcher's knowledge of context, decision to use an established theoretical framework or interest in a particular subject or theme. However, the selection of features can also involve a more data-driven approach where certain principles, separate from any specific research purposes an analyst may have, are used to highlight patterns in the data.

Such an approach is represented by the use of corpus linguistic methods. When used to support the analysis of discourse, corpus linguistics refers to a set of procedures that can be applied to a large body of 'electronically encoded texts'; that is, a corpus (Baker, 2006, p. 1). It involves using software and statistical or frequency measures to calculate results that reveal distinct linguistic features of a corpus and therefore also the discourse it represents. These features – for example, collocates (words that tend to co-occur at a rate greater than would be expected by chance) or keywords (words statistically more frequent in one corpus when that corpus is compared to another corpus, often one containing a similar but different text type) – can then be used to direct a closer qualitative analysis of text samples.

Corpus-assisted approaches have been used in a number of previous studies on online grooming discourse (e.g., Schneevogt et al., 2018; Lorenzo-Dus et al., 2020; Lorenzo-Dus and Kinzel, 2021; Evans and Lorenzo-Dus, 2022; Lorenzo-Dus, 2023). In the present work, findings from an analysis of the LE dataset using corpus linguistic methods are included in Section 4, where these are relevant to the theme of 'power'. Keywords were calculated for sub-corpora of LE, one consisting of the conversational turns of groomers and the other of child-targets, using PAN2012 as a reference corpus and the statistical measure log likelihood. Seven salient keywords, the same for each sub-corpus, were selected from the top thirty for close analysis. For this purpose, concordances – multiple lines of the same searched item displaying text to the immediate left and right – were reviewed: 100 random concordances for each keyword and each sub-corpus. The concordances were then allocated to thematic categories based on inferences made about their meaning and function, and the percentage of each category for each keyword compared across the sub-corpora.

With the research presented in this Element, complementarity is central to the approach we have taken. We use a mix of methods that fall under the general umbrella of discourse analysis, including frameworks identified above (e.g., speech act theory and politeness theory). Given that these vary between the empirical sections that follow, we have included specific methods at the start of two of the sections, Sections 3 and 5, while the approach to power in Section 4 is explained by the theory on power as it relates to manipulation (discussed in Section 2.2) and the account of discourse analysis provided in this section.

3 Online Grooming As Language Action

3.1 Introduction

Example 3.1

01	Child	Promises are HUGE TO ME. So don't promise unless you
02		mean it

This example is part of a female child's response to a male adult who is grooming her online. The grooming adult's promises of spending time together, and her reply in Example 3.1, occur in the context of their discussing their 'relationship', which the groomer has framed in primarily romantic terms. The groomer's behaviour is morally and legally reprehensible. It constitutes manipulation (cloaking sexual abuse as romantic love) and fits the criterion of the offence of sexual communication with a child (see Section 1). Crucially for this section, the example illustrates a well-established view of language as action (as performative), whereby language shapes as well as reflects reality. Within language performativity, the example also illustrates the difference, as postulated in speech act theory (see Section 3.2), between

(i) what we say;
(ii) what we mean by what we say; and
(iii) the uptake of what we say by those we communicate with.

In Example 3.1 the child's utterance (here, what she types – (i)) is intended as an instruction (the intention behind the typed-up turn – (ii)) to the grooming adult she believes herself to be romantically involved with to stop making empty promises to her. Her instruction is a Directive speech act (see Section 3.2), worded as a command (note the use of the imperative mode – 'don't promise', line 01). The child supports her instruction with a reason, namely the importance she assigns to the speech act of making a promise ('Promises are HUGE TO ME.

So . . . ', line 01). This is emphasised through lexical and typographical choices: selecting a superlative adjective ('HUGE', line 01) and typing it – and the self-referential cataphor ('TO ME', line 01) – in capital letters, respectively. The child's turn also entails 'facework', specifically politeness (see Section 3.2). The red heart emoji ('❤', line 02)[15] following the directly worded, emphatically grounded instruction simultaneously serves as a 'negative'- and 'positive'-oriented 'politeness strategy' (Brown and Levinson, 1978/1987): as mitigation of the potential face-threat against the grooming adult of her expressing her instruction via an imperative and as affirmation of her interest in (i.e., her romantic feelings towards) him, respectively. Regarding (iii), the child's speech act in Example 3.1 may – or may not – result in the groomer refraining from making such promises in the future.

In this section we explore this performative dimension of language in relation to online grooming, mobilising tenets of speech act and (im)politeness theory. Although reference is made to children's language use, the analysis focusses on performativity in groomers' goal-driven communication. Section 3.2 provides a brief account of those tenets in speech act and (im)politeness theory that are directly relevant to the analysis. Section 3.3 identifies and describes how groomers' goal-driven discourse is articulated in a number of manipulation tactics. This is followed, in Section 3.4, by an examination of speech act realisation in online grooming discourse, and of how – in the case of groomers – speech acts and tactics align. Section 3.5 offers some conclusions that point to the analysis of power dynamics (Section 4) and child communicative behaviour (Section 5).

3.2 Online Grooming As Performative Discourse

The case for an action-based approach to language has been argued within various disciplines, in particular from the second half of the twentieth century onwards. For instance, in the 1960s Roman Jakobson (1960/1985) proposed an influential theory of communicative functions of language that comprised six functions: referential, emotive, conative, phatic, metalingual and poetic. Only the referential function concerns language as an exchange of information; the remaining five incorporate some language-as-action dimension.[16] Jakobson's theory was instrumental in challenging the view that language simply reflects reality.

[15] In the original message the emoji appeared in red.

[16] The 'conative' function refers to relationships between speakers and what language achieves in this social realm; the 'poetic' function attends to the aesthetic dimension of linguistic form and how it links to specific effects; the 'emotive' function attends to the kind of effects that the expressive and subjective aspects of talk can have; the 'phatic' function refers to the role played by ritualised communication; and the 'metalingual' or 'metalinguistic' function refers to how language can reflect on itself, including the role it plays in social interaction.

The work of another highly influential linguist of the twentieth century, namely the ordinary-language philosopher J. L. Austin, was also centrally concerned with the performativity of language. In *How to Do Things with Words*,[17] Austin (1962) argued that language consists of a series of speech acts by means of which speakers and hearers achieve things communicatively. This became known as speech act theory (SAT). Any speech act involves – as introduced through Example 3.1 – three facets:

(i) The *locution*, which is the act of saying something. In Austin's words, this 'includes the utterance of certain noises [the phonetic act], the utterance of certain words in a certain construction [the phatic act], and the utterance of them with certain "meaning" in the favourite philosophical sense of that word, i.e., with a certain sense and with a certain reference' (1962, p. 92);
(ii) The *illocution,* which explains the reason for which a speaker is using the locution; that is, 'for asking or answering a question, giving some information or an assurance or a warning', and so on (1962, p. 98); and
(iii) The *perlocution*, which is the effect of what was said: 'the perlocutionary act always includes some consequences, as when we say "By doing x I was doing y"' (1962, p. 107).

Perlocution is arguably the most controversial aspect of SAT, with some scholars arguing that it falls outside the remit of SAT altogether. For example, four decades ago, Geoffrey Leech stated that 'perlocutionary effects do not form part of the study of pragmatics, since pragmatic [illocutionary] force has to do with goals rather than with results' (1983, p. 203). More recently, Kurzon's (1998) study of the speech act of inciting concluded that perlocutionary acts are 'outside the domain of speech act theory' and called for the replacement of the term perlocution with 'uptake' (1998, p. 595).

When it comes to cyber-crime legislation, perlocutionary effects appear to be secondary to the locution/illocution aspects of speech acts. The sexual communication with a child offence referenced earlier is an enshrinement of the performativity of language use. Importantly, it does not require such communication to result in the intended (perlocutionary) effect. Nor does it require the illocutionary force to be part of sexually explicit locution. Similarly, since 2019 UK counter-terrorism legislation incorporates the communicative encouragement of terrorism, regardless of the 'uptake' such encouragement may have, and

[17] Austin's work originally developed as a series of lectures delivered at Harvard University in 1955 and was posthumously collected and published in the 1960s. For detailed accounts of speech act theory's tenets, evolution and critique, among other considerations, see, for example, Allan (1997).

not just overt textual calls to commit terrorist acts (Macdonald and Lorenzo-Dus, 2021). This takes us to another important paired concept in SAT: direct–indirect speech acts.

Let's take the example of promising, with which this section started. Earlier in the interaction the groomer said 'I promise', marking his intention via an explicit performative (a performative verb) in which he expressly stated that he was performing the speech act of promising. This constitutes a direct speech act. At other points he did not expressly state his intention via a performative verb, using instead indirect speech acts; for instance, 'I'll always love you'. Austin's (1962) concept of 'felicity conditions' is relevant here; that is, the conditions that need to be satisfied for a speech act to be successful, for its function to be fulfilled. As Searle (1969/1975, p. 68) further notes, 'I may only say "I'll do it for you"'. That utterance (the locution act) 'will count as and will be taken as a promise in any context where it is obvious that in saying it I am accepting (or undertaking, etc.) an obligation'. With certain speech acts we routinely skip use of the performative verb. In the case of promises, this may be because the verb is often used in the colloquial phrase 'I promise you' with the meaning of 'I assure you', which does not involve a speech act of promising – as in Searle's (1969/1975, pp. 58–9) example: '"You stole that money, didn't you?", "No, I didn't, I promise you I didn't"'. In other cases, use of a performative verb is simply not possible. As Kurzon (1998, p. 585) argues in relation to the speech act of inciting,

> there is no illocutionary verb *incite* that enables us to say (31a), or even (31b):
>
> (31a) *I incite you that the bank is easy to rob.
> (31b) *I incite you to rob the bank.
>
> So in order to incite, the speaker in fact does not incite! That may sound paradoxical, but such is the case.

Incitement entails using different illocutionary acts, such as making statements, promises and requests. But, as Kurzon (1998, p. 35) notes, there is 'not one act which may be glossed as "to incite" – One may argue that the statement "I incite you to make an explosive" is syntactically possible, but in practice S [speaker] is very unlikely to incite by making such a statement'.

Indirect speech acts tend to carry more persuasive force than direct acts. Marc Antony's ironic funeral oration is an oft-cited example (see, e.g., Barendt, 2009). When requesting something of others, indirectness may help to mitigate any perceived imposition on them and thus tend to their 'negative face needs' (Brown and Levinson, 1978/1987). In so doing, indirectness may also address our own face needs as speakers (Searle, 1975). Moreover, indirectness may contribute to underline common ground between speaker and hearer, which helps to address the hearer's 'positive face needs' – that is, the need to feel liked and appreciated (Brown and Levinson, 1978/1987) – and/or to construct the speaker's identity (Terkourafi, 2011). These benefits are well understood by advertisers and politicians, among others. In cyber-crime contexts, including grooming, indirect speech acts are of particular practical importance as they lend themselves well to the regular use of covert manipulation (see Lorenzo-Dus, 2023 and Section 2). Groomers may see communicative indirectness (and hence their use of indirect speech acts) as reducing the likelihood that the child will notice their manipulative intention and therefore also reducing the risk that the abuse will be disclosed. This explains in part groomers' frequent use of vague language when expressing sexual intent (Lorenzo-Dus and Kinzel, 2021). Moreover, as noted earlier, some speech acts may hardly ever – indeed never (e.g., inciting) – be realised directly. Promises and requests are usually indirect – the hearer must often draw inferences to understand the speaker's meaning.

3.3 Online Groomers' Goal-Driven Communication

Research into online grooming has examined offender behaviour, deriving criminogenic and psychological profiles (e.g., Elliott and Beech, 2009; Gottschalk, 2011; Webster et al., 2012; Martellozzo, 2013; De Hart et al., 2017; Seto, 2019). Research has also identified factors that may determine a child's 'vulnerability level' to becoming a victim of online grooming (e.g., Whittle et al., 2014; Kloess et al., 2017). However, most of the research into online grooming has been devoted to identifying and classifying its components, both in terms of what these are and their interrelations. As a result, there exist several 'online grooming models'. These mainly account for groomer intentions/goals,[18] such as friendship development, risk assessment and so forth (see, e.g., O'Connell, 2003; Williams et al., 2013; Kloess et al., 2017; Winters et al., 2017; Joleby et al., 2021; Powell et al., 2021; van Gijn-Grosvenor and Lamb, 2021). And, in most of them, such intentions/goals are derived from content and thematic analyses of, often, a subset of PJ chat logs and, in some cases, interviews with convicted offenders.

Linguistically informed models of online grooming are more recent and limited, with notable exceptions being Lorenzo-Dus et al. (2016, 2020), Chiang and Grant (2017, 2018) and Lorenzo-Dus (2023). As introduced in Section 2, Chiang and Grant (2017, 2018) used genre analysis in their work. They examined twenty digital sexual grooming chat logs from PJ (2017) and

[18] Different terms are used, for example 'themes', 'strategies' and so forth.

one LE transcript of an offender interacting with several children (2018). Their combined analyses identified sixteen rhetorical moves used by groomers.[19]

For their part, Lorenzo-Dus et al. (2016) applied a digital discourse analysis (Herring, 2013) framework, supported by relational work (Locher and Watts, 2008), to a dataset comprising twenty-four PJ chat logs. The analysis led to their positing an online grooming discourse model, comprising three phases ('access', 'entrapment' and 'approach'). The entrapment phase entailed four 'processes' ('deceptive trust development', 'sexual gratification', 'isolation' and 'compliance testing'), some of which encompassed a number of 'strategies' (e.g., 'mental isolation' and 'physical isolation'). In a subsequent study, applying a corpus-assisted discourse studies (CADS) methodology to the analysis of the entire PJ dataset, Lorenzo-Dus et al. (2020) validated the 2016 model. The authors noted concerns about the performance across the extended PJ dataset of one of the entrapment processes, namely 'compliance testing', which designated groomers' checking probability of a child engaging in whatever activity the groomer proposed. A revised model that also incorporated analysis of LE chat logs was proposed in Lorenzo-Dus (2023), which Figure 1 schematically represents. A definition of the tactics in the model, and the sub-tactics of some of them, is presented in Table 1.

The model in Figure 1 includes the following revisions:

(1) The previous terminology (phase, process and strategy) is replaced with just one term (tactic). This reduces terminological complexity in the previous model and emphasises, through the term 'tactic', the sense of careful planning to achieve specific ends; that is, the manipulative essence of online groomers' goal-driven discourse;
(2) All the tactics are embedded within an all-encompassing entrapment network, as opposed to keeping 'access' and 'approach' as, respectively, linear entry and exit points. As shown in Figure 1, 'access' surrounds the entire online grooming practice and 'approach' is better conceptualised as regular attempts to secure further engagement with the child, online and/or offline, that occur throughout their grooming interaction, hence it being re-labelled as a FC tactic; and
(3) 'Compliance testing' is replaced with the broader notion of facework, which applies to the entire grooming discourse practice. This reflects the finding that groomers' gauging of a child-target's level of acquiescence happens throughout their grooming relationship, and it is therefore aligned to all the groomer tactics.

[19] The sixteen moves were: greeting, maintaining conversation, meeting planning, reprimanding, sign-off, rapport, assessing likelihood and extent of engagement, assessing criteria fulfilment, assessing and managing risk, assessing role, sexual rapport, initiating sexual topics, maintaining/escalating sexual content and immediate sexual gratification; and (added in their 2018 paper) overt persuasion and extortion.

Table 1 Groomer tactics and sub-tactics

Tactic	Sub-Tactic	Definition
Access (A)		Groomers' use of language to contact children and engage them in conversation.
Deceptive Trust Development (DTD)	Activities	When groomers attempt to build a sense of familiarity and commonality with children by talking about different kinds of activity. They do this by engaging children in talk about hobbies and interests or eliciting and sharing information about ongoing and planned activities.
Groomers' use of language to bond with a child to help them achieve their main goal of engaging the child in sexual activity	Exchange of Personal Information (EPI)	When groomers elicit and provide personal information to engage children in a process of getting to know each other.
	Praise	When groomers compliment or congratulate children as a way of developing and maintaining good relations with them.
	Relationships	When groomers engage children in discussion about romantic and/or sexual relationships with others, and/or the groomer, in order to build a close personal connection.
	Small Talk	When groomers engage in informal conversation with no obvious communicative goals for the purpose of making children feel comfortable talking to them while keeping a conversation flowing.

Table 1 (cont.)

Tactic	Sub-Tactic	Definition
Sexual Gratification (SG)	Explicit Sex Talk	When groomers seek to desensitise children to sexual acts by using sexually explicit language that may be accompanied by sexually explicit images/media.
Groomers' use of language to involve children in sexual activities online and/or prepare them for sexual interaction offline	Implicit Sex Talk	When groomers seek to desensitise children to sexual acts through sexually implicit language.
	Reframe	When groomers use language to position themselves and children in roles intended to persuade children that sexual activity, including sexual talk, is beneficial to them.
Isolation (I)	Mental Isolation	When groomers attempt to make children feel emotionally disconnected from their support network and more emotionally dependent on the groomer. This can serve the purpose of discouraging children from telling others in their support network about the grooming relationship, thus reducing the risk – for groomers – of their abuse being discovered.
Groomers' use of language to separate children from others in their support network, especially friends and family	Physical Isolation	When groomers attempt to interact with children away from others, in situations where the child is available to engage in sexual activity and discovery of abuse is less likely. This can involve checking if a child is alone, encouraging them to physically separate from their support network and

Table 1 (cont.)

Tactic	Sub-Tactic	Definition
		getting them to delete digital traces of their interactions with the groomer.
Further Contact (FC)	Online	When groomers try to gain longer or new periods of online interaction with children or try to establish different ways of communicating with them. The purpose of this is to create more opportunities for online grooming.
Groomers' use of language to get children to provide an increased amount or type of contact	Offline	When groomers try to get children to meet with them in person for the purpose of engaging them in sexual activity.

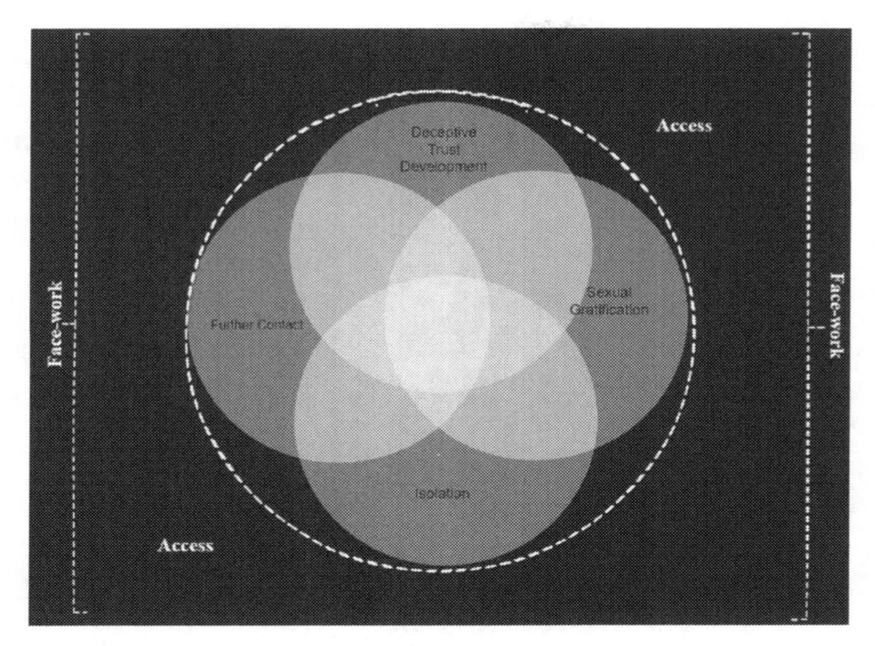

Figure 1 A model of online grooming discourse (groomer-focussed)

As Figure 1 visually illustrates, groomer tactics are non-sequential rather than always following some linear practice that may start with DTD, develop into I, progress into SG and end in requesting an in-person meeting (FC offline). Also, groomer tactics overlap. For instance, the Praise sub-tactic supports the DTD tactic – the groomer expresses their liking for some child feature, which contributes to creating an affective bond and, hence, to trust building for deceptive purposes. Yet, groomers' use of the Praise sub-tactic also supports the SG tactic (when praising/complimenting the child on sexually oriented topics/features) and the Mental Isolation sub-tactic (when praising/complimenting is presented as groomer views about the target that others close to them are unable to appreciate).

Figure 2 shows the frequency of use of groomer tactics in the LE dataset, alongside the equivalent use in Lorenzo-Dus et al. (2016), which examined PJ groomer data.

The results are evidently very similar.[20] In both datasets, the main tactic is DTD, which accounts for slightly over half of all the tactics (51.99 per cent in the LE dataset; 53.33 per cent in the PJ dataset), followed by SG, which

[20] Space limitations preclude breaking the results down at the sub-tactic level, where the patterns are also similar.

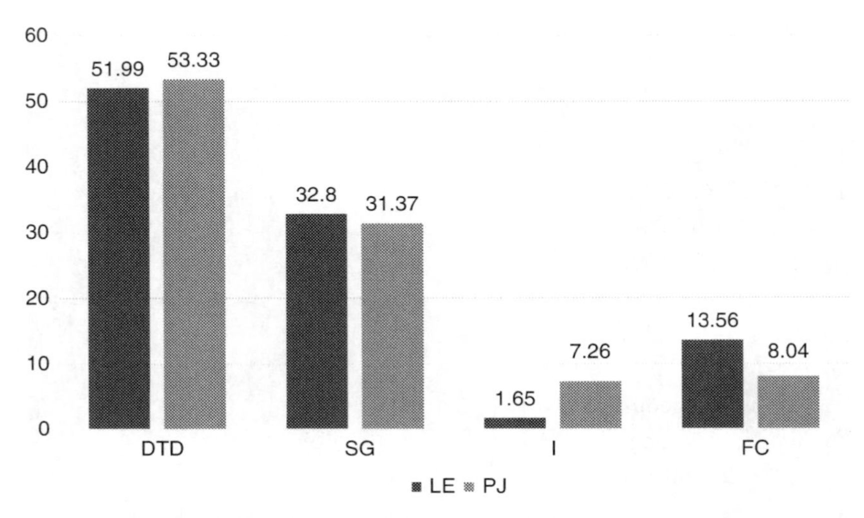

Figure 2 Tactics in online groomers' discourse (per cent)

accounts for just under a third of the total use of tactics by groomers in the LE (32.8 per cent) and the PJ (31.37 per cent) dataset. The two other tactics are, comparatively speaking, less frequent in both datasets – at 13.56 per cent of the total in the LE dataset, FC is the only other tactic with > 10 per cent frequency of use. Despite their low-percentage use, the FC tactic is more frequent comparatively than the I tactic, although the difference between them is minimal in the case of the PJ dataset (8.04 per cent FC; 7.26 per cent I) and more marked in the case of the LE dataset (13.56 per cent FC; 1.65 per cent I). Overall, the results support the Lorenzo-Dus et al. (2016, 2020) model with the revisions stemming from its application to the LE dataset. The results confirm the comparative salience of talk that seeks to build trust for deceptive purposes in online grooming, which has important implications for prevention-/detection-oriented efforts that may not focus on this tactic, favouring the SG tactic instead. This is not to say that talk that seeks to desensitise a child to sexual activity, as per the SG-Explicit, the SG-Implicit of the SG-Reframing sub-tactics, is unimportant. Indeed, frequency-based results are not the panacea to developing online grooming countering solutions, an argument applicable to all the tactics. Infrequent and/or even single tactic occurrence can still lead to groomers' perlocutionary effect of manipulating children. While providing a useful overview of the 'tactical orientation' of groomers' discourse, the results in Figure 2 must be further interrogated. Section 3.4 does so from a language-as-action perspective.

3.4 A Speech Act Theory-Informed Analysis of Online Grooming Discourse

SAT provides a useful lens through which to examine how groomers deploy their tactical, goal-driven manipulation. This is because (sub-)tactics can be linguistically realised in different ways, including through different speech acts (the illocutionary force of which may be directly/indirectly expressed), making use of different (im)politeness strategies and so forth. For instance, groomers typically perform the Praise sub-tactic via direct compliments. Compliments, such as those oriented to sexual topics, may in turn be sexually explicit (e.g., 'What a babe ;) Them blowjob lips :P') or implicit (e.g., 'Your gorgeous, I think your sooo pretty + hot') and they may (not) be accompanied by negative politeness strategies (e.g., 'hope u don't mind me saying'). Compliments may also be paid in their own right (as the main speech act for the Praise sub-tactic) or serve as facework (positive politeness strategies) in support of other (sub-)tactics, which are themselves realised via other speech acts. A compliment may, for instance, be a grounding move in support of an SG tactic performed via an explicit sexual Directive (see Section 3.4.1), such as 'Omg ur so sexy u can undo my zip and take off my bottoms off babe xxxx'. In other words, speech acts reflect and shape particular groomers' (sub-)tactics that are aligned to specific goals/intentions and that, overall, contribute to groomers' manipulation of children for sexual abuse.

In the remainder of this section, we analyse speech act use in online groomers' discourse, comparing it to children's use of speech acts also during online grooming. Then we examine groomers' use of speech acts per (sub-)tactic. The analysis is conducted on a corpus of thirty-six online grooming chat logs (~50,000 words; thirty-six different groomer–child dyads).

Our speech act analysis is informed by Searle's (1969/1975, 1978) taxonomy of illocutionary speech acts and its adaptation to OCSEA datasets by Grant and Macleod (2020). Searle's illocutionary acts' classification includes the following categories:

- Assertives: acts that commit a speaker to the propositional truth being expressed. They can be affirmative (e.g., 'I've just had dinner') or negative (e.g., 'I have not eaten yet') – in both cases they are statements that may be labelled 'true' or 'false'.
- Directives: acts that are meant to result in the hearer taking a specific course of action. They range in terms of in/directness: commands are the most direct, hints are the most indirect and requests (themselves including different realisations) are in the middle.

- Commissives: acts that commit a speaker to a future action, such as threats, offers and promises.
- Expressives: acts that express a speaker's emotions or attitudes about a given subject, such as thanking and apologising.
- Declarations: acts that alter the state of things by being uttered (i.e., performatives in Austin's (1962) terms).

Grant and Macleod (2020) consider Interrogatives (questions) separately, rather than as a type of Directive, which is how they are classified in Searle's taxonomy: as requests for information. Their rationale for doing so in the context of OCSEA data analysis is also applicable to our analysis: Interrogatives 'are pivotal to the maintenance of "Relationships over IM [Instant Messaging – the data examined]" [. . .] questions are one of the most frequent methods for introducing new conversational topics' (Grant and Macleod, 2020, p. 42). The authors also add an 'Acknowledgements' speech act category to account for 'Many turns within the IM chat [that] appeared to be performing the singular action of (minimally) acknowledging an interlocutor's prior turn'. Again, given the similarity in datasets, we also include this category in the analysis presented here.

Our analysis yielded a total of 4,994 (groomers) and 2,635 (children) speech acts. Figure 3 shows how these were distributed in the data. It is worth noting the following:

- No instances of Declarations were identified (as was also the case in Grant and Macleod (2020), hence they are not included in Figure 3;
- Commissives were further coded as threats, offers or promises. This was on account of the debate in the online grooming literature regarding offender use of (non)coercive communication styles, specifically threats (see, e.g., Chiang and Grant, 2018; Schneevogt et al., 2018; Lorenzo-Dus and Kinzel, 2019, 2021; Joleby et al., 2021; Lorenzo-Dus, 2023); and
- Expressives were also broken down into thanking, apologising and, as proposed in Grant and Macleod (2020, p. 42), emojis/emoticons. While there were many instances of emoji/emoticon use (and written representations of laughter) in our data, no instances were identified of their being used in isolation as Expressives, as opposed to in support of other speech acts, which is why they are not represented in Figure 3.

As Figure 3 shows, Assertives were the most frequent category used by groomers (42.71 per cent – 34.41 per cent affirmative, 8.3 per cent negative) and, especially, by children (61.99 per cent – 45.01 per cent affirmative; 16.98 per cent negative). In both cases, affirmative Assertives (34.41 per cent for groomers; 45.01 per cent for

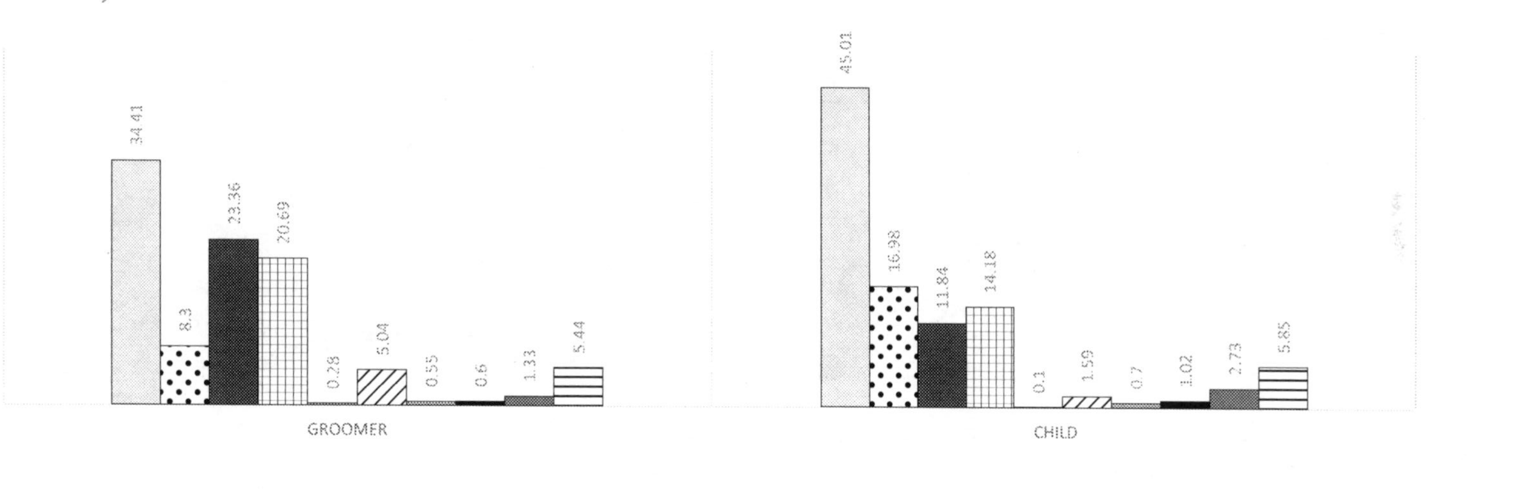

Figure 3 Speech acts in online grooming (per cent)

children) were more frequent than negative Assertives (8.3 per cent for groomers; 16.98 per cent for children). Directives and Interrogatives were the two other most proportionally frequent speech acts for groomers and children. Groomers used Directives and Interrogatives more frequently (23.36 per cent and 20.69 per cent, respectively) than children (11.84 per cent and 14.18 per cent, respectively), with children performing Interrogatives slightly more frequently than Directives and groomers showing the inverse trend. The remaining speech acts displayed considerably lower frequencies of use, all of them being under 10 per cent of the total (for groomers and children) and, given space constraints, are not discussed in detail here. It is worth noting, though, that the main groomer–child difference for those less frequently deployed speech acts concerned the percentage figure for offers by groomers (5.04 per cent), which more than doubled that for children (1.94 per cent). In performativity terms, then, online grooming may be described as an activity type (Levinson, 1979) that is saliently built around the speech act of exchanging information for groomers and children (via Assertives); and also around the speech act of instructing children by groomers (via Directives) and of seeking information of groomers by children (via Interrogatives). The more frequent use of Directives by groomers than by children supports the argument – developed in Section 4 – that online grooming entails a power imbalance that does not favour children.

To gain a more nuanced interpretation of the results in Figure 3, we examined how the three most frequent speech acts – Assertives (affirmatives and negatives), Directives and Interrogatives – were aligned to groomers' use of (sub-)tactics. This entailed manual mapping of each speech act to one or more groomer (sub-)tactics. The results of this analysis are shown in Figure 4.

As discussed in Section 3.4.1 (Figure 3), Assertives were particularly frequent in groomers' discourse. Figure 4 shows that over half of all these speech acts (56.04 per cent affirmative Assertives; 53.77 per cent negative Assertives) were aligned to DTD sub-tactics, especially the DTD-Relationships sub-tactic (19.99 per cent affirmative Assertives; 30.82 per cent negative Assertives). Assertives were also frequently used in relation to SG-Explicit (19.99 per cent affirmative Assertives; 16.99 per cent negative Assertives) and SG-Implicit (13.23 per cent affirmative Assertives; 13.11 per cent negative Assertives). There was no other sub-tactic in which Assertives displayed a >10 per cent frequency.

Groomer use of Interrogatives was most frequently aligned to the DTD-Relationships (17.01 per cent) and SG-Explicit (16.91 per cent) sub-tactics, followed by the DTD-Sociability (13.78 per cent), DTD-EPI (12.8 per cent), SG-Implicit (12.61 per cent) and DTD-Activities (12.22 per cent) sub-tactics. Their use of the other sub-tactics was infrequent: < 5 per cent in all cases. As noted in

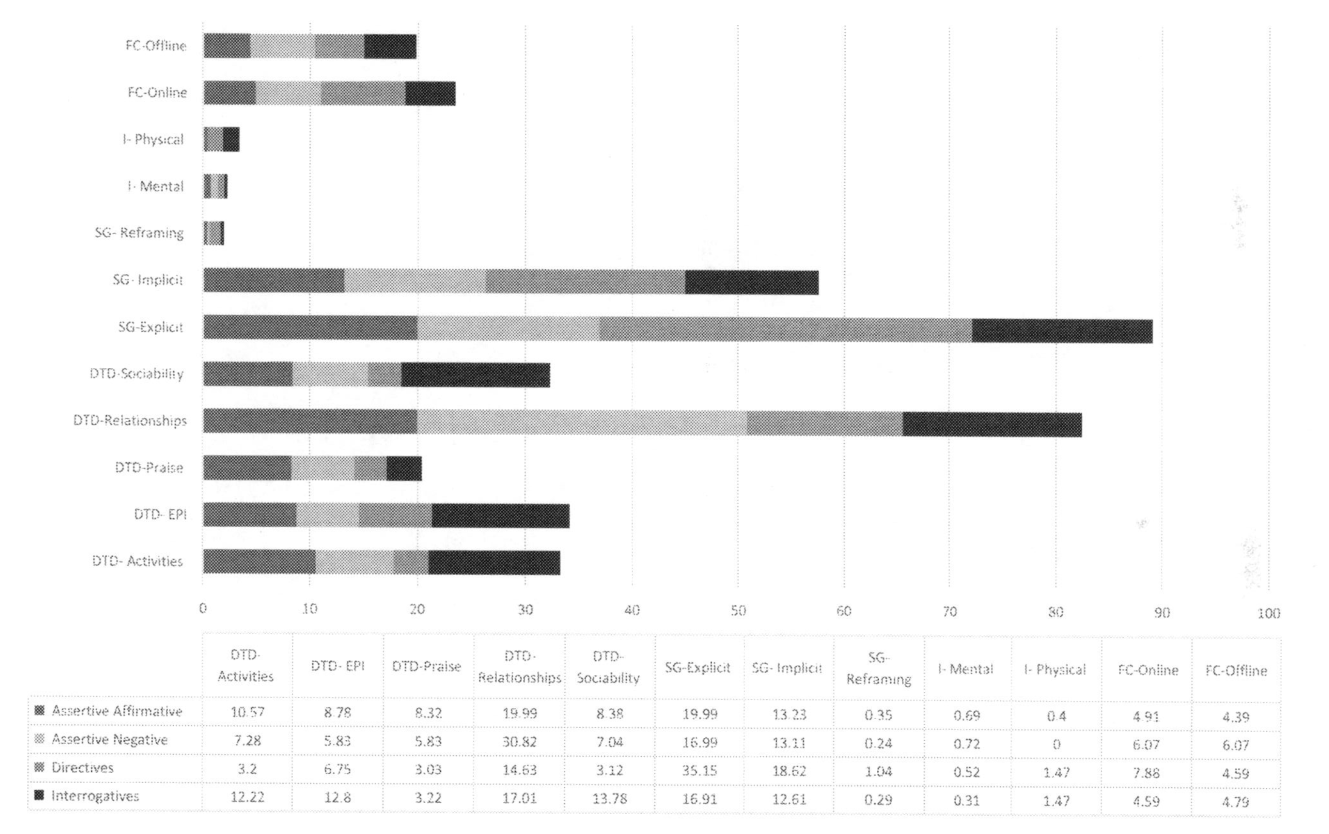

	DTD-Activities	DTD- EPI	DTD-Praise	DTD-Relationships	DTD-Sociability	SG-Explicit	SG- Implicit	SG-Reframing	I- Mental	I- Physical	FC-Online	FC-Offline
Assertive Affirmative	10.57	8.78	8.32	19.99	8.38	19.99	13.23	0.35	0.69	0.4	4.91	4.39
Assertive Negative	7.28	5.83	5.83	30.82	7.04	16.99	13.11	0.24	0.72	0	6.07	6.07
Directives	3.2	6.75	3.03	14.63	3.12	35.15	18.62	1.04	0.52	1.47	7.88	4.59
Interrogatives	12.22	12.8	3.22	17.01	13.78	16.91	12.61	0.29	0.31	1.47	4.59	4.79

Figure 4 Speech acts and sub-tactics (per cent) in groomers' discourse

Section 3.2 (Table 1), many of the DTD sub-tactics concern some form of information exchange, such as personal details, pastimes, relationships with boy/girlfriends and so on. As per the principle of communicative reciprocity (or reciprocal disclosure), one may expect a combination of Assertives and Interrogatives being most frequently aligned to the sub-tactics of DTD-Activities, DTD-EPI and DTD-Relationships. Assertives, as we have seen, were frequently used in these sub-tactics. Yet the comparatively higher use of Interrogatives in these DTD sub-tactics suggests that DTD is more about manipulative, one-way (groomer–child) questioning than about reciprocal, groomer–child disclosure. This supports the view of online grooming as being far from a level playing field, communicatively or otherwise, as discussed in Section 4 in the context of groomer–child power relations.

Groomers used Directives most frequently to perform the SG-Explicit sub-tactic (35.15 per cent), followed by the SG-Implicit sub-tactic (18.62 per cent). Combined, the SG tactic was aligned to over half (53.33 per cent) of all the Directives used by groomers in the data under analysis. The salience (35.15 per cent) of explicitly worded instructions for children to engage in some form of sexual behaviour further supports the argument that online grooming is characterised by imbalanced power dynamics – especially given that most of these sexually explicit Directives deployed most direct head acts (i.e., commands).

Space limitations preclude a detailed analysis of the actual realisation of Directives in the sample under consideration. In this regard it is, however, instructive to consider the results of Lorenzo-Dus' (2023) analysis of groomer Directives (n=119) in a corpus of ten online grooming LE chat logs. The analysis was informed by Blum-Kulka et al.'s (1989) framework and entailed coding for

(1) participatory perspective (i.e., whether Directives were speaker (groomer), hearer (child) or third-person (generic) oriented);
(2) head act realisation, including level of in/directness therein; and
(3) supporting moves of different kinds, such as groundings, hedges, boosters and so on.

The analysis found more than half of the Directives to be aligned to the SG tactic. Regarding (1), over two-thirds of the Directives were hearer-oriented; that is, the child was the subject in the grammatical clause containing the head act (e.g., 'can you do x?'). As for (2), there was a balance across the sub-tactics between directness (mainly use of imperatives and want statements), which accounted for just under half of all the Directives, and indirectness (use of conventional indirectness formulae, i.e., query preparatories such as 'can you . . . ?'), which accounted for the remaining Directives. The only exception was the SG-Explicit sub-tactic, in which head act types were primarily oriented towards directness, most often imperatives. Given that these directly worded Directives constitute illegal and immoral sexual behaviour, groomers may likely assume that the children may interpret them as face-threatening. Yet no effort, in the request head act at least, was made in these cases to mitigate their face-threat level.

This is not to say that child-oriented facework was altogether avoided. Indeed, and regarding (3), Lorenzo-Dus' (2023) analysis identified regular, strategic use of facework (positive *and* negative politeness strategies) in most of these Directives. This, she argued, is indicative of broader self-styling and stance-taking in online groomers' discourse, whereby groomers regularly integrate use of politeness strategies, on the one hand, and impoliteness on the other, moving swiftly across them (Lorenzo-Dus, 2023). In the case of Directives aligned to the SG tactic, for instance, the head act may be direct, such as a mood derivable (a direct command to perform a sexual act on camera), *and* contain several grounding moves that attend to the child's positive face needs (e.g., a compliment about the child's physical/sexual appearance; references to their close relationship, etc.) and negative face needs (e.g., use of hedges, such as 'just once'), to minimise the perceived imposition on the child of the command being performed. If the child hesitates, politeness strategies may quickly be dropped and replaced with impoliteness, such as use of conditional threats (e.g., 'if you do (not) do x, I will (not) . . . '). This pivoting between 'nice and nasty talk' is cognitively complex for a child to make sense of and may be one of the reasons why a child may find 'stop' strategies (see Section 6) hard to deploy.

Returning to Figure 4, the only other sub-tactic within which Directives were used > 10 per cent is DTD-Relationships (14.63 per cent). This entailed groomers seeking to get children to take a specific action regarding their romantic and/or sexual relationship with each other or, as illustrated in Example 3.2, other people in the children's life.

Example 3.2
[The groomer and the child are discussing the child's relationship with her boyfriend.]

01	Groomer	That should happen, you should break down, it harms your
02		self-esteem etc
03		Trust me
04	Child	I trust you

In lines 01–03 the groomer uses a Directive to manipulate the child into breaking up with her boyfriend. The 'head act' in this Directive ('you should break down', line 01) is supported via two related 'grounding moves' that express disapproval in general ('That should [not] happen', line 01) and specific (child-related) terms ('it harms your self-esteem etc', lines 01–02). These grounding moves serve as positive politeness strategies that seek to make their recipient, here a child who has previously shared that she is unhappy with her boyfriend, feel liked and appreciated. These moves therefore support interpersonal bonding and, through that, trust building. The latter aspect is indeed explicitly acknowledged in the groomers' reinforcement head act ('Trust me', line 03), which seems to have the intended perlocutionary effect on the child ('I trust you', line 04).

Finally, it is important to consider a regular feature of groomers' use of speech acts across (sub-)tactics, given its potential perlocutionary effect on children, namely fixated discourse. This entails groomers communicatively pursuing actions insistently, without a similar level of interest from their target (Egan et al., 2011). Fixated discourse is linked to groomers' performance of a 'child-target avidity stance' – that is, an extreme focus on the child they are grooming that they disguise as genuine interest rather than manipulative abuse (Lorenzo-Dus, 2023). In facework terms, fixated discourse constitutes a form of harassment – specifically encroachment-based impoliteness (Culpeper, 2011). Let's consider Example 3.3.

Example 3.3

01	Groomer	Please
02		Please
03		I didn't mean it
04		Come on
05		Hi
06		Sorry
07		Hello?
08		Hi

Lorenzo-Dus (2023) shows that groomers' fixated discourse can be self-oriented (narcissistic talk) and/or other-oriented – to the child they target (harassment) or to their perceived opponents (persistent questioning about, e.g., the child's parents). In Example 3.3, the groomer's speech acts are varied: an implicit apology ('I didn't mean it', line 03), an explicit apology ('Sorry', line 06), an emphatic (through repetition of the booster 'please') Directive to be forgiven ('Please', 'Please', 'Come on', lines 01, 02, 04) and a request for FC ('Hello?', line 07), supported by a friendly/informal greeting ('Hi', line 08). The apologies are self-oriented; the other speech acts are child-oriented. Altogether, they entail eight consecutive conversational turns that receive no reply at all from the child, indicating fixated discourse on the groomer's part.

3.5 Conclusion

Online grooming provides a performative context of communication in the truest sense of Austin's (1962) 'doing things with words' dictum. It is not just talk – let alone harmless fun, as it is sometimes presented by groomers. Although online grooming and other forms of technology-assisted CSEA are sometimes viewed as less serious than offline CSEA (for a discussion, see Hamilton-Giachritsis et al., 2021), their emotional, psychological and behavioural outcomes appear to be just as harmful, with specific and still little-understood impacts on children (Hamilton-Giachritsis et al., 2020). That being the case, and given our starting premise that online grooming relies on *communicative* manipulation (Section 2), this section has examined the performativity of language in online grooming through the lenses of SAT.

Having described the (sub-)tactics used by groomers, the analysis focussed on the kind of speech acts that groomers and children deploy most/least frequently during online grooming, and how – in the case of groomers – these speech acts align to particular (sub-)tactics. The results show that online grooming is more about sharing information (via affirmative Assertives, especially) than it is about seeking it (via Interrogatives) or about instructing action (via Directives), although those two speech act realisations also feature relatively frequently – and more so in the discourse of groomers than in the discourse of children. The results also show that groomers' speech acts are most frequently aligned to sub-tactics that revolve around relationship building (DTD-Relationships) and explicitly seeking sexual pleasure (SG-Explicit).

This finding is consistent with accounts by those with lived experience of online grooming that groomers cloak sexual abuse as romantic love – something that is cognitively and affectively very complex for children to process and can thus delay or prevent disclosure as part of possible recovery journeys (see, e.g., Whittle et al., 2013; Hamilton-Giachritsis et al., 2017; Mullineux-Morgan and Lorenzo-Dus, 2021, 2023). Groomer speech acts are often direct, and persistent, as the results in this section also show. This can only make it more challenging for children to develop 'resistance' strategies, especially if under pressure to engage (to reply, to provide CSAM, etc.) in (almost) synchronous time. As we will see in Section 4, the situation is further complicated by the marked power asymmetry in online grooming, which means that power is disproportionally one-directional (groomers have much more than children) even if communication is bi-directional, as will be discussed in Section 5.

4 Power in Online Grooming Discourse

4.1 Introduction

In online grooming interactions, and as shown in Example 4.1, groomers sometimes use forceful language when attempting to induce children to engage in sexual activity with them.

Example 4.1

01 Groomer: Right, I can't be arsed anymore. Are we going to cam and
02 both do stuff or not
03 dont waste time, dont change subject ffs:P

Frustrated by what they perceive to be the child's evasiveness, the groomer in this example issues an ultimatum for the child to either perform sexually on camera ('cam and do stuff', lines 01–02) 'or not' (line 02). A sense of urgency to act is created by the repetition of imperatives in quick succession, instructing the child to not delay and pressuring them to make a decision ('dont waste time, dont change subject', line 03); specifically, to choose the ultimatum's first option or risk the groomer – who they may feel emotionally invested in – ending the conversation ('Right, I can't be arsed anymore', line 01).

At other times, groomers employ friendlier approaches when tempting children to participate in sexual activity, as Example 4.2 illustrates.

Example 4.2

01 Groomer: I love to cuddle. It would feel great to snuggle up to you
02 What you wearing right now?
03 Child: Nothing
04 Groomer: Oh? Give me a peek under the sheets?

In this example, the groomer expresses preference/liking ('I love to cuddle', line 01) and desire ('It would feel great to snuggle up to you', line 01) rather than making demands. The groomer also frames sex as romantic physical contact ('snuggle up', line 01) and engages in a flirtation routine by asking about the child's current state of dress ('What you wearing right now?', line 02) before fishing for them to share a nude image of themselves ('Give me a peek', line 04).

Whether it involves groomers aggressively imposing their will on children or subtly encouraging them to comply with their needs, as corresponds to the use of impoliteness or politeness strategies, respectively (see Section 3), online grooming is about power: about how adult groomers use language to exercise power over the children they target. In this section, we address the question: what is the role of power in enabling adults to sexually groom children? To answer this, we build on the discussion of manipulation as relates to power in

Section 2 (Section 2.2) and the research findings presented in Section 3 regarding groomer manipulation (sub-)tactics, taking a broader approach to examine groomer–child power relations: both in terms of how these are already established in the context of a pre-existing adult–child power differential and how they are performed through the way groomers and children use language when interacting with each other.

The section starts with an examination of groomer discursive power, presenting and discussing findings with a focus on explicit power in Section 4.2 and implicit power in Section 4.3. Section 4.4 discusses a distinct realisation linked to implicit power – power-based sexual roleplaying – before focussing on the counteraction of groomer power, child resistance (Section 4.5 – see also Section 5), and then summarising the section and providing some reflections in the conclusion (Section 4.6).

4.2 Explicit Power in the Talk of Online Groomers

As noted in Section 2.2, a power differential pre-exists any interaction between groomers and children: as an adult, the groomer has more access to power resources (e.g., knowledge, experience, certain legal rights, status, etc.) than a child. This greater power of online groomers compared with the children they target often manifests in the way they both use language when interacting with each other. Sometimes groomer displays of power are bald, as in Example 4.3, in which a groomer pressures a child to engage in sexual activity.

Example 4.3

01	Groomer:	lets do it ok?
02	Child:	I'm shy though see
03	Groomer:	just do it
04		the best way to get over it
05		is just doing it
06	Child:	I know
07	Groomer:	well lets get on with it
08		you said you'll prove to me
09		so prove
10		come on
11		I've given loads of chances

The groomer expresses force by taking turns without reply – where the turns represent the same sought action (an example of fixated discourse; see Section 3) – and repeatedly using imperatives ('do it', line 03; 'get on with it', line 07; 'so prove', line 09; 'come on', line 10), including in the same form more than once ('do it', lines 01 and 03). The groomer's insistent language creates a sense of urgency for the child to comply with their demand, and though the child initially resists several turns after those presented in Example 4.3 ('just leave it'), further similar insistence from the groomer eventually results in the child's compliance: 'I will do it because I like you I need to prove it'. In facework terms, the groomer's communicative behaviour is impolite (Culpeper, 2011). At the same time, and also in facework terms, the imperatives in the groomer's Directive speech act are softened by use of positive politeness strategy of including speaker (groomer) and hearer (target) in the same activity (Brown and Levinson, 1978/1987), here via the inclusive 'lets' (lines 01 and 07), and the negative politeness strategy of minimising the size of the imposition (Brown and Levinson, 1978/1987), here via the hedging adverbial 'just' (line 03). This facework, combining impoliteness and (positive and negative) politeness, illustrates a characteristic of groomer discourse, namely pivoting between 'nice and nasty talk', as introduced in Section 3. It also suggests that the groomer is taking a stance of expertise (see Lorenzo-Dus, 2023); specifically, here the groomer adopts the persona of a coach using 'tough love' to support a pupil lacking in confidence. The child's minimal responses and agreeability ('I know', line 06) show that the groomer is being successful in this manipulative dynamic.

The explicit power of the groomer in Example 4.3 is also expressed through their use, in quick succession, of several different language devices for manipulation purposes. These include representing the desired sexual action as beneficial to the child's personal growth, which corresponds to the manipulation sub-tactic of reframing ('the best way to get over it . . . is just doing it', lines 04–05); representing the child's action or inaction as a moral obligation – that is, the morality around fulfilling one's promises ('you said you'll prove to me', line 08); and strategically presenting the situation as one in which the groomer is the imposed-upon party ('I've given loads of chances', line 11). Groomers' use of aggressive and pressuring language likely represents either a strategic escalation of their attempts to manipulate children or an expression of their frustration at having not achieved sexual gratification up to that point in a grooming interaction.

Another way that groomers exercise explicit power through their talk is by taking the lead in their conversations with child-targets, as Example 4.4 illustrates.

Example 4.4

01	Groomer:	what you like on here
02	Child:	jst chatting with people there nicer here than at school
03	Groomer:	what you chat about
04	Child:	dnt mind really 😀
05	Groomer:	you have boyfriend

06	Child:	nah i used to 😃
07	Groomer:	what happened
08	Child:	dunno he jst dumped me ☹

In Example 4.4, the groomer controls the interaction by asking – in the style of an interrogation – a series of quickfire questions that positions them as the receiver and the child as the provider of information and allows the groomer to dictate the conversation in terms of topic and tone. This use of questions suggests an explanation, at least in part, for the finding presented in Section 3.4.1 that Interrogatives are comparatively more frequent in the discourse of groomers than children. By asking questions, groomers can gather the kind of personal information that they might be able to exploit when trying to groom a child, such as the fact the child may not have good relations with their peers ('people . . . nicer here than at school', line 02) and that they have experienced romantic rejection ('jst dumped me', line 08); these reflect the groomer's use of the I tactic and the Relationships sub-tactic, respectively (see Section 3.2).

The power of the groomer in this exchange also, to some extent, represents an effect of the child's apparent willingness to follow the groomer's lead. Throughout the conversation from which Example 4.4 is taken, the child answers the groomer's questions but without asking or introducing any topics of their own.

Groomers' tendency to take on the role of conversational leader is not only evidenced by their more frequent use of Interrogatives, but also by their greater likelihood to start new conversational sequences compared to children. Manual identification of all instances of the start of new conversational sequences aligned to tactical communication in the LE corpus (details of the method used are provided in Section 5.4) shows that groomers overwhelmingly start more sequences than children do, as shown in Figure 5. This is with the one exception of sequences linked to the Exchange of Personal Information sub-tactic of the DTD tactic (see Section 3), which represents the kind of balanced exchange one might expect in power-symmetrical interactions between two individuals. However, in the case of topics linked to all the other (sub-)tactics, groomers are the primary initiators, which represents the imbalanced nature of power-asymmetrical interactions that are characteristic of online grooming.

The discussion of Example 4.4 highlighted the link between asking questions and the greater power of groomers, which suggests that the high occurrence of Interrogatives may be a distinctive feature of groomer discourse. This is further suggested by the fact that 'what' is a keyword in a sub-corpus representing the talk of groomers, where it is used 80 per cent of the time to ask questions.[21] Its role in

[21] Identified by reviewing 100 random concordance lines of 'what' (see Section 2.3.3 for details).

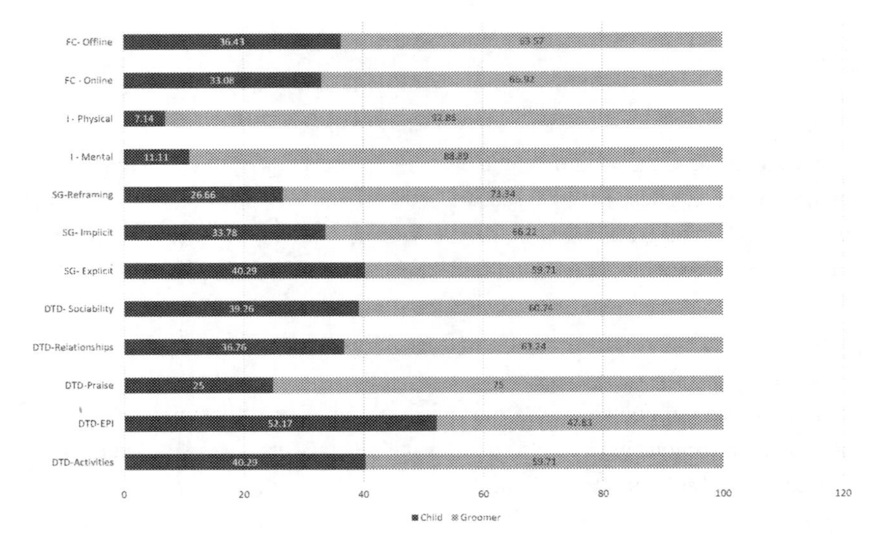

Figure 5 Conversational sequence/tactic 'start' (per cent) by children and groomers

driving forward interactions with children and eliciting information to support grooming has already been illustrated in Example 4.4, where the groomer uses 'what' three times to ask questions that support the performance of several DTD sub-tactics.

'What' is also a keyword in a sub-corpus representing the talk of child-targets (see Section 2). Despite this, it can still indicate groomer power, as this keyword is used differently by groomers and children. A close examination of the concordances of 'what' reveals that, while it serves similar functions in the talk of groomers and children, there are differences within these. For example, when 'what' is used to inquire about activities (17 per cent of the time by groomers, 12 per cent by children), groomers use it more to elicit specific information (e.g., 'What you doing after school'), when employing the DTD sub-tactic Exchange of Personal Information, and child-targets use it more to make general conversation (e.g., 'What you up to'). This corroborates the finding, as seen in Figure 5, that groomers tend to dictate topics of conversation. It also suggests that groomers monitor a child's social activities (as per the DTD sub-tactic Activities) and, therefore, the possibility that they are engaging in controlling behaviour.

While the keyword 'what' can represent a feature of power in the talk of online groomers, this is only with respect to the particular way it is sometimes used. The word itself does not represent a marker of power. This is because it has many other functions that do not signify power, as illustrated by the fact that 'what' is a keyword of the talk of children. Even so, in this section we have demonstrated ways in which power is explicit in online grooming discourse, which suggests the possibility of other words or phrases serving as markers of groomer power.

Indeed, power markers in online grooming warrant further investigation. However, there are several reasons why such markers may be hard to identify in the discourse. These include the potential for considerable variation within and between different grooming interactions, with respect to the language style of individual groomers, the stage of the grooming process and the relationship between groomer and child. Each of these factors is likely to affect how groomers choose to perform power through their talk. Another reason is that explicit power is not always expressed by single words or phrases but rather through the way words are used in combination, as with fixated discourse (see Section 3) when otherwise innocuous words or phrases are repeated in close succession (e.g., the request 'call me', or greeting formulae, as seen in Example 3.3) to create a pressuring, and even intimidating, effect. The lack of clear markers of power in the talk of groomers can also be attributed to the fact that online grooming often involves the disguise of power, as discussed in the next section.

4.3 Implicit Power in the Talk of Online Groomers

Groomers' overt performance of power when using aggressive language or taking the lead in conversations with children they are grooming may be intended to induce compliance in the children. However, signalling the power differential between groomers and children in this way promotes social distance and risks reducing the groomer's influence on the child. This is likely a calculated risk taken by groomers who are confident in their dominance over a child, which may come from the grooming process being sufficiently advanced, or a child's communication being submissive from the outset of a grooming interaction. Although displays of power are part of their tactical armoury, more common is the tendency for groomers to try to mask the greater power they possess compared to the children they target. This can take the form of groomers hiding social indicators of power such as age (they may pretend to be younger than their actual age) or adopting a stance of 'vulnerability openness' (Lorenzo-Dus, 2023), whereby they disclose information and emotions that make them come across as being in a weak position, as Example 4.5 illustrates.

Example 4.5

01	Child:	talk to me? bet u sound good
02	Groomer:	nooo 😉 I'm shy with talking 🤭

The groomer's claim to be 'shy with talking' (line 02), supported by the use of an emoji indicating embarrassment ('🤭', line 02), is contradicted by recurrent instances, represented in the data, of the same groomer encouraging spoken communication when interacting with other children (e.g., 'can u hear me ... put earphones in'). Yet this is not to say that they intend to represent themselves as entirely lacking in confidence. When purporting to be vulnerable and non-threatening (the effect created by the shyness claim in this example), the groomer's stance-taking is tactical: to lull the child into a false sense of security in the groomer not representing a danger. However, the groomer is careful not to completely put off the child, as shown by their use of a winking face emoticon/emoji when resisting the child's request to talk ('nooo 😉', line 02), which expresses a playful attitude and suggests a willingness to negotiate.

Sometimes groomers attempt to disguise the groomer–child power imbalance by emphasising the choice and agency of the child. In doing so, and as Example 4.6 shows, they create an impression of the child as being in control and not at the mercy of the groomer's dominance.

Example 4.6

01 Groomer: ... its up to you not me 🙂 Just thought you would watch me or
02 you'll do a little 😉 😛

That the groomer immediately follows up the assertion about the child's free will ('its up to you not me', line 01) by trying to guilt them into engaging in sexual activity highlights how it has been said for effect rather than meant sincerely. Here, the groomer states their expectation of the choice the child would make ('watch me or ... do a little 😉 😛', lines 01–02). By using negative politeness – the hedges 'just' (line 01) and 'a little' (line 02) and the conditional tense ('you would watch', line 01) – to convey that it is a small thing to expect, the groomer insinuates that the child is behaving unreasonably if they decide against engaging in such activity.

In Example 4.6, the groomer's token representation of the child's power contrasts with their own active power as they attempt to assert their influence on the child's decision-making. However, groomers' disguise of the power imbalance in their interactions with children is often more subtle. This is the case when they take on the persona and register of a friend or peer and use language in a way that suggests a conversation is taking place between social equals, which Example 4.7 illustrates.

Example 4.7

01 Groomer: Whats your favourite to cook x
02 Child: Risotto but only because that's like one of four things I can
03 make from memory
04 Groomer: Oh cool i love it x
05 Child: My dad taught me xx
06 Groomer: Oh cool mum taught me x

By asking the child about their preferences in relation to an everyday activity like cooking, thereby using the DTD sub-tactic Activities (see Section 3), the groomer acts as if they are interested in the child as an individual and not just as a target for achieving sexual gratification. They adopt a conversational register characteristic of how close friends might communicate. This is represented by their use of the easy-going expression of acceptance 'Oh cool' (lines 04 and 06) and the phrase 'i love it' (line 04) to express enthusiastic appreciation of the child's response to their question. The use of positive politeness here is likely intended to make the child feel good about talking to the groomer, while the groomer mirroring the structure and content of the child's sharing of personal information ('dad taught me/mum taught me', lines 05/06) represents 'reciprocal disclosure' (see Section 3.4.2) and creates an effect of fluid concord and them both engaging in a natural, smooth exchange. Structure/content mirroring is also illustrated by the use of the letter 'x' to represent kissing in lines 04–06.

The groomer's goal in this interaction is to bond and build trust with the child-target in order to make them more susceptible to their influence and control. In this way, it represents a power move, though one that is implicitly exercised through the DTD tactic. The language itself is indistinguishable from what might be expected to be used in a conversation between friends, and therefore is likely to require knowledge of context (that is, the fact that one of the participants is a groomer) for it to be interpreted as a deception. This makes the nature of the power exercised particularly insidious and hard to detect.

Implicit power in online grooming discourse refers not only to manipulative deception but also to how patterns in the language choices of groomers and children can index pre-existing power differences. An example of when language use indexes power is provided by previous research on the speech act of apologising, where power status has been identified as a variable for determining when and how people apologise (Holmes, 1995). Here, one rationale for the link between power and apologising is that people with low power status who cause offence are more likely to experience negative social consequences than people with high power status.

In the context of online grooming, groomers' efforts to disguise their greater power by taking on the persona of a friend suggest they are likely to apologise just as often as children, whereas other evidence of groomers overtly performing power suggests they may be likely to apologise less. In fact, 'sorry', a word strongly associated with the act of apologising, is a keyword in the talk of groomers and children within the LE dataset, and a review of concordances reveals that groomers and children use it equally often for relationship repair work – in the case of groomers, this represents use of the Relationships sub-tactic (see

Section 3). A possible explanation for 'sorry' occurring as a keyword is that grooming represents a relationally volatile situation. The different goals of groomers and children – the former primarily seeking sexual gratification, the latter often seeking a romantic relationship – create a high potential for disagreement but also a strong incentive for both to want to reconcile when conflict occurs.

An unexpected finding from the concordance[22] analysis of 'sorry' is that 10 per cent of the time it is used by groomers to absolve children of the need to apologise (e.g., 'don't be sorry it's fine'). Although a relatively small percentage, 10 per cent is not insignificant given the tendency for the word 'sorry' to usually refer to the attitude of the speaker or writer. Also, the data shows that children did not use 'sorry' for the same purpose, suggesting that when used in this way 'sorry' may in fact index groomer power. This is in the sense that through their readiness to tell children not to be 'sorry', groomers show their greater authority as someone in the role of directing interpersonal dynamics in a conversation.

4.4 Power-Based Roleplaying

In the previous section we observed how groomers sometimes try to disguise power differences by emphasising the idea that the child is in control. This is central to a manipulative practice often employed by groomers within the SG tactic: that of inducing children to engage in power-based sexual roleplay, where the child is assigned a domineering role and the groomer adopts a submissive role. Groomers' attempts to engage children in sexual roleplay are illustrated by Example 4.8.

Example 4.8

01	Groomer:	so i'll cam soon yeah? what do u want me to do as a little
02		show? and then u got to tell me everything then yeah?
03	Child:	erm
04		strip
05		and touch yourself
06		dunno the rest yet need to think
07	Groomer:	I'm already naked :P
08		touch myself? u mean wank?
09	Child:	ohh
10		and yeah sort of

Here, the groomer takes on the role of sexual performer ('what do you want me to do as a little show?', lines 01–02) while instructing the child to take on the domineering role of sexual director ('u got to tell me everything', line 02). By driving forward the roleplay in this way, the groomer expresses their authority,

[22] 'Concordance' is defined in Section 2.3.4.

which is also reflected in the child's compliance as they immediately begin to issue commands ('strip . . . touch yourself', lines 04 and 05) in line with the role assigned to them. Any power associated with a child giving orders in an induced sexual roleplay performance is superficial. This fact is clearly evident in Example 4.8, where the child repeatedly expresses hesitancy ('erm . . . dunno . . . sort of', lines 03, 06 and 10) while the groomer, adopting a stance of expertise (Lorenzo-Dus, 2023), uses correcting ('I'm already naked', line 07) and clarifying ('touch myself? u mean wank?', line 08) comments to coach them on how to play the part. The controlling influence of the groomer is obvious in this particular example, but the nature of reversed-power roleplay means that it is usually hidden behind the way the child uses language to act as if they are in control.

Inducing children to participate in sexual roleplay is clearly manipulative: not only does it realise the groomer goal of engaging a child in sexual activity, but it does so in a way that disguises groomers' abusive behaviour and reduces the risk of this being discovered or disclosed. If a third party was to read/review a chat log representing a groomer–child sexual roleplay interaction, they might perceive the child as an active participant. This could cause them not to recognise that CSA is taking place, especially if they lack understanding of the manipulative context. As for the child, being manipulated to take on the domineering role of telling the groomer what to do sexually may make them feel that they are jointly culpable (along with the groomer) for an illicit act rather than, as is in fact the case, the victim of a sexual offender.

Groomers also use induced sexual roleplay as a ploy to escalate children's involvement in sexual activity. They do this by initially assigning them a role where the child is only required to give orders and not to have to perform any sexual acts themselves, as was illustrated in Example 4.8. This exploits the sexual curiosity of a child and may encourage them to feel that they can engage in consequence-free fun. However, after completing their performance, the groomer will sometimes turn the tables and urge the child to now take on the role of submissive sexual performer, as shown in Example 4.9.

Example 4.9

01	Child:	don't have to do anything anymore x
02	Groomer:	your turn 😉
03	Child:	noooo
04	Groomer:	think u should 😉
	. . .	
05	Groomer:	get ready slave 🤭
06		your turn

07 come on obey me
08 I want to see ur ass, now.
09 Child: you never said anything about me being the slave

In this example, the groomer repeatedly uses an elided affirmative Assertive ('your turn', line 02, line 06) to convey the illocutionary force of a Directive speech act. This gives the claim for a returned sexual performance from the child, the force of a statement of fact making it seem like something unquestionably owed. Initially, the groomer uses relatively low modality[23] ('think u should 😉', line 04) to urge the child to reverse roles, but then switches to using Directives, the head acts of which – imperatives ('get ready', line 05; 'come on obey me', line 07) and a want statement ('I want to see ur ass', line 08) – are direct and used to express a more insistent attitude. Potential face-threats caused by the groomer's suddenly pushy behaviour are mitigated by their use of language indicating the roleplay register ('slave', line 05; 'obey', line 07) to suggest that they may be in character. In line 09 the child protests the groomer's efforts to get them to take on a submissive role: 'you never said anything about me being the slave'. While they might not submit to this particular attempt, the groomer's efforts are still likely to create in the child a sense of obligation and being in debt to the groomer.

The power-based nature of sexual roleplay in online grooming contexts is sometimes crystallised by certain terms of address, such as 'mistress', 'slave' and 'daddy'. 'Mistress' always refers to the child and 'daddy' to the groomer, while 'slave' can refer to either. Although primarily used by groomers, they also occur in the talk of children, which probably represents them mirroring groomers' usage. An effect of using these naming devices, one likely intended by the groomer, is that they encourage children to feel emotionally and psychologically disconnected from any sexual activity. They do this by representing an exaggeration of the roles they denote and by emphasising the idea of such sexual activity being a game; that is, a playful pretence that is not completely real and therefore does not cause any actual harm to the child. While the terms 'slave' and 'mistress' are used in routines where power roles are subverted, 'daddy' seems to confirm power differences, and in a way that suggests an incestuous paedophilic fetish. Here, the groomer's use of this word may be intended to exaggerate an inappropriate type of relationship in order to treat it with knowingness, perhaps as an in-joke, and obscure the sense in which it actually represents abuse.

[23] Modality refers to language that expresses obligation, possibility, likelihood and so on, and the strength of these can vary depending on word choice (e.g., compare 'could', 'should' and 'must').

4.5 Child Power: The Language of Resistance

Power, both pre-existing and that exercised through discourse, is central to how adults are able to sexually groom children. That is why our focus so far in this section has been on groomer power. However, children are not simply passive receivers of groomers' abusive actions: they have agency and make choices that can, to varying degrees, represent a realisation of their own power. As shown in Section 4.5, the appearance of a child being in control when interacting with a groomer may in fact represent induced sexual roleplay and the power of the groomer. In this way, the only child action that can be reliably interpreted as an exercise of power in grooming contexts is that which clearly serves their interests and, therefore, involves resistance (see Section 5 for a broader discussion of this communicative behaviour). Child resistance to online grooming is demonstrated whenever they use language to try to end a particular line of conversation or the entire interaction with a groomer, as illustrated by Example 4.10.

Example 4.10
01 Child: I don't want to speak to you anymore.

By using clear and direct language to reject the groomer, the child displays an impressive clarity of feeling and purpose. Children who have been subjected to groomer manipulation are likely to experience feelings of confusion, especially if they are emotionally invested in the groomer but resistant to being pressured to engage in sexual activity with them. Such emotional uncertainty is likely to cause children to express their resistance in far more subtle and ambiguous ways than that shown in Example 4.10.

One way is suggested by another finding from the analysis of the keyword 'sorry' in the LE corpus. In 21 per cent of uses by groomers and 33 per cent of uses by children, 'sorry' functions as an apology for interruptions or absences. The greater tendency for children to use it in this way could be explained by the fact that it might sometimes represent a subtle expression of resistance. For example, when a child says 'sorry ... I just keep getting distracted', their intention may be to let the groomer know that they are not a priority in the child's life. Such temporary withdrawals from grooming interactions arguably represent acts of resistance by children to the influence of groomers, allowing them to feel in control but without completely ending contact with the groomer.

Child resistance represents a kind of self-power that children exercise when using language to maintain control over their life choices and to protect themselves from harm. This can be demonstrated in a clearcut way, as illustrated by the child's rejection of a groomer in Example 4.10. However, whether a child's behaviour represents resistance in interactions with groomers is often open to interpretation and can require assumptions to be made about their intentions or feelings. This is the case when a child unexpectedly ends contact with a groomer without explanation, as Example 4.11 illustrates:

Example 4.11

01	Groomer:	wtf?
02		all good, then were about to cam and u delete me
03		grow up

There are several possible interpretations of the child's sudden withdrawal from the conversation here. One is that, on recognising the danger posed by the person they are talking to online, they decide to cease all interaction in order to protect themselves from being manipulated were the conversation to continue. Another is that the child feels intimidated by the groomer's attempt to escalate the interaction by involving a camera for the purpose of sexual performing. Either way, ceasing contact arguably represents an act of resistance and, therefore, a performance of self-power in that the child is making a choice to keep themselves safe.

Even though the child in Example 4.11 ends the conversation, the final power move may belong to the groomer when they express bafflement ('wtf?' – line 01) and use an impoliteness strategy, age-related condescension ('grow up' – line 03). In doing so they convey that, by deleting the groomer as a connection on the online platform, the child is behaving irrationally, and that this behaviour can be attributed to their immaturity. This could potentially have a negative effect on the child's self-esteem, especially if it plays on the insecurity experienced by many children about wanting to be taken seriously. In this way, children's resistance to the harmful influence of groomers is not necessarily just achieved by the act of ending contact but may also depend on *how* they end that contact.

As shown in Example 4.10, one way for a child to assert their power is by using language to express an outright rejection of the groomer. However, this is not the only way, as illustrated in Example 4.12 where the child uses sarcasm to resist the groomer's advances.

Example 4.12

01	Groomer:	Whats the secret to being so gorgeous then
02	Child:	dunno early bedtimes?
03	Groomer:	haha :L

In this example, the groomer's tongue-in-cheek use of a clichéd pick-up line (line 01) is likely intended to elicit an appreciative response from the child by complimenting them on their appearance but doing so in a playful manner (an effect emphasised by use of the tongue sticking out emoji (😜, line 01)) to get them to engage in a flirtatious routine. In reply, the child comes back with their own dismissively sarcastic question ('dunno early bed-times?', line 02), implicitly rejecting the groomer's compliment by making an obvious pretence to interpret their question literally. The effect is one of resisting the groomer's attempt to hook them but in a sarcastically humorous way that avoids impoliteness, with the possible perlocutionary effect of provoking an angry reaction from the groomer. By using sarcasm and humour, the child not only performs resistance but does so in a way that neutralises the groomer by showing them that they are impervious to their influence. The conversation ends after the groomer represents laughter in their response ('haha :L', line 03), indicating that the child has been successful in deterring them while avoiding face-threat.

4.6 Conclusion

In this section, our account of power in online grooming discourse has primarily focussed on the talk of groomers, though we have also considered child power, specifically resistance to grooming. Our examination of how groomers and children's power is reflected and performed in discourse has included looking at examples of grooming interactions. Through these, we have not only identified features of power but also presented evidence of the power dynamics when groomers interact with children.

A main finding from the research reported in the current section is that groomer power is realised in many ways. Power explicit in the discourse can take several forms, such as expressed forcefulness or groomers taking the lead in interactional management. When power in the discourse is implicit, it often involves the use of subtle manipulation tactics where outward expressions of power are either hidden, as occurs with the DTD tactic, or exaggerated in order to disguise the actual power being exercised, as occurs in sexual roleplaying within the SG tactic. Groomers' ability to influence children is also largely supported by the power imbalance that already exists between the two. However, groomer power is not always left unchecked, and children employ a variety of discursive means to resist groomers. In this section, we have highlighted some features of child resistance and the effect of these on child–groomer power dynamics, though there remains scope for further research on how these may change over the course of a grooming interaction.

The complexity of power in online grooming and the myriad forces that shape groomer power vis-à-vis the child, as shown in this section, highlights the scale of the challenge in knowing when, and understanding how, someone a child is talking to online may be trying to influence them in a harmful way. As noted in Section 1, a key missing piece in research, and arguably practice approaches to date, is a close analysis of children's communication in grooming interactions. Attention to date has focussed on groomer language, which effectively silences children's voices. Section 5 examines children's communication, exploring how linguistic analysis can support a closer attunement to children's experiences and amplify their voices to achieve a more holistic understanding of how power, agency and victimhood intersect in online grooming.

5 Dismantling Agent/Victim Dichotomies: Children's Discourse during Online Grooming

5.1 Introduction

How is a child supposed to behave when they are being manipulated by a groomer? There is growing recognition of the problems for child safeguarding caused by the tension between notions of an 'ideal victim' (Christie, 1986) and narratives of children engaging in 'risky behaviour', making 'active lifestyle' choices or, in the case of OCSEA, failing to 'keep themselves' safe online and adhere to safety advice. Binary agent/victim dichotomies have been shown to impact on the levels of support that children receive, leading to documented shortcomings in identifying and responding to some cases of CSE (see, e.g., Jay, 2014; Ofsted, 2014, 2016; Hallett, 2017; Beckett, 2019). These dichotomies are argued to be rooted in a 'failure to recognise, and work with, the potential co-existence of both agency and constraint, both harm and gain' (Beckett, 2019, p. 24). An illustration of child communication that may not match expectations about the behaviour of an 'ideal victim' is provided by Example 5.1.

Example 5.1

01	Child	what kinds of thing you like to do?
02	Groomer	anything.. I don't care if i don't like it i'll still do it.. not bothered me 😏
03		so the question is what do you like
04	Child	i love getting lists of kinky things for me to choose from 😏

In Example 5.1, the child appears to be taking an active leading role in a conversation about sex, one already introduced by the groomer, by asking a question about the groomer's sexual preferences: 'what kinds of thing you like to do?' (line 01). The groomer responds by expressing a willingness to engage in any kind of sexual activity ('anything', line 02), and does so in a way that conveys a carefree attitude and suggests that an openness to sex is a positive character trait: 'I don't care . . . not bothered me 😏' (line 02).

This sets up the groomer's attempt to prompt the child to express a similar attitude: 'so the question is what do you like' (line 03). In their response, the child reflects the groomer's interest in sex but, in contrast to the groomer's submissive tone ('if i don't like it i'll still do it', line 02), the child indicates that they like to be in control ('i love getting lists of kinky things for me to choose from 😉', line 04). In this example, we see the child communicating with the groomer and exerting a degree of choice and agency in pursuit of their own communicative goals, although these are constrained and moulded by the groomer's tactical and power-abusive communication (see Sections 3 and 4).

This section seeks to bring new focus to children's communication in grooming interactions, addressing a major gap in research on online grooming discourse, which has prioritised groomer language (see Section 2). The imperative to identify and understand criminal behaviour has led to the dominance of groomer-centred approaches that have resulted in children's communication being largely overlooked. This section contends that the only way to achieve an accurate and nuanced understanding of online grooming is to dismantle dichotomies of children being either victims or agents by raising children's voices through the study of their language.

In the next section (Section 5.2), we discuss victim/agent dichotomies with reference to existing debates in relation to CSEA that reverberate throughout OCSEA. This helps explain the need for a nuanced and sensitive account of child discourse in online grooming contexts and is followed, in Section 5.3, by a brief review of research that has addressed child discourse in these contexts. Section 5.4 reports and discusses findings from the analysis of child discourse in the LE dataset (see Section 2). Finally, Section 5.5 reflects on how our findings relate to the broader need to pay more attention to the language and voices of the child victims of online grooming.

5.2 Children's Discourse Online: Reconciling Victimhood and Agency

Digitally mediated communication pervades modern life. This is particularly significant for children, whose early relationships are central to their socialisation, development of communicative competence and ability to make sense of their place in the world (Kidron et al., 2018; NSPCC, 2020; Ofcom, 2022). While the digital age means that children have more opportunities to explore and shape their identity, it also exposes them to greater risk as many digital spaces lack adequate regulations and protections. Recognising the increased opportunity for children to have agency in an online world, but without a corresponding increase in safety measures, reverberates with debates among child-safeguarding researchers and practitioners about issues of victimhood and agency, consent and constraint, and the implications of victim blaming, for children who experience sexual exploitation and abuse (Sidebotham, 2013; Beckett, 2019; Pearce, 2019; Taylor, 2020; Dodsworth, 2022).

The increased agency and risks for children online builds on an already problematic perspective of CSEA, based on a dichotomous conceptualisation where children are viewed as either agent or victim, and therefore either blamed or seen as in need of rescue (Dodsworth, 2022). The origins of this dichotomy lie in the mid-1990s with the emergence of a new discursive formation of children as 'victims of abuse' (Melrose, 2010, 2013a) that 'managed to negate the idea that the child might, in any way, exercise agency' (Melrose, 2013a, p. 159).

Critics of this victim/object construction argue that it results in a harmful, individualistic perspective, whereby the issue is reduced to one of individual morality/immorality, creating a perspective of a homogenised victim. It is a perspective that skews policy and practice focus towards 'individual redemption', often placing the onus on the child to change their behaviour (Pearce, 2009, p. 253; see also Beckett, 2019). Individualising victimhood occludes an ecological systemic view that takes in wider familial, socio-economic, educational, health and housing factors (Hallett, 2016, 2017; Dodsworth, 2022).

We concur with the argument that agency and blameless victimisation are not mutually exclusive. Rather, they co-exist and are most usefully understood together (Sidebotham, 2013; Hanson and Holmes, 2014; Hanson, 2019; Dodsworth, 2022). As Beckett (2019, p. 34) emphasises: 'the choice we see in many situations of CSE is one that is highly constrained and externally influenced. It does however exist, and a failure to recognise this will lead to continued overlooking of potential harm in situations where the child may appear and/or feel themselves to be in control'. This sees children who experience CSEA as having the capacity to 'evaluate circumstances, identify goals and preferred options (albeit from a possibly limited palette), and implement steps to pursue them' (Beckett, 2019, p. 34). However, crucially, this capacity is bound by a complex set of constraints that operate at multiple levels and are unique to a child's individual circumstances (Beckett, 2019). There is growing recognition that the key is thus to move towards a greater appreciation of the existence of multiple realities, deferring to the validity of the diversity of people's experiences and exploring ways to gather the 'stories of lived lives' (Reinharz and Davidman, 1992; Dodsworth, 2022, p. 291). An untapped resource to access these stories and experiences is the study of children's synchronous communication in OCSEA contexts.

5.3 Children's Discourse in the Context of Online Child Sexual Abuse and Exploitation

While there is a growing body of research eliciting accounts of children's lived experiences of online grooming, including those involving the use of surveys (e.g., Finkelhor et al., 2009; Wolak and Finkelhor, 2016; Villacampa and Gómez, 2017), semi-structured interviews and focus groups (e.g., Quayle et al., 2012; Davidson et al., 2016; Hamilton-Giachritsis et al., 2020), there remains very little research looking at the language used by children during grooming interactions.

Where transcripts of real-life online child sexual grooming interactions have been used, research has tended to focus on the groomer's rather than child's communicative behaviour. In the very limited work in which the language of real children is present in the data, the focus has remained on how this affects groomer behaviour. For example, Chiang and Grant (2018) have suggested that threats and coercion are more forceful when groomers interact with real children rather than decoys. However, there is an acknowledged scarcity of research analysing both the child *and* the groomer's communicative behaviour to explore, for instance, how threats are built up, communicated and managed by both interactants (Seymour-Smith and Kloess, 2021), although some research does acknowledge the merits of studying both groomer and child communication in interaction (Kopecký et al., 2015; Kloess et al., 2017; Kopecký, 2017). In Kopecký (2017), child blackmail cases were analysed, and the results of the analysis used to propose a model of child blackmail and extortion. However, although the stated aim of the study was to develop a model to predict the communication of the offender and the child, the proposed model focussed on the groomer's communicative behaviour without close attention to the child's own communication or detailed analysis of their response to the blackmail.

In Kloess et al. (2017), a thematic analysis was carried out of transcripts of chat logs between offenders and children via internet platforms. The stated aim was to explore the phenomenon of sexually exploitative communication from the child's perspective. The study examined children's behaviour and responses when approached by offenders and identified a variety of vulnerability factors present within the children in the sample. However, the authors make a dubious distinction between those children apparently engaging in interactions for reasons of curiosity and sexual exploration/experimentation and those that represented 'serious' offences of sexual abuse. Despite this, the authors' conceptualisation of a continuum of children's negative experiences online is helpful, as is their recognising the need to frame exploration and discussion of the child's perspectives and agentive decisions in online grooming interactions.

In another study, Seymour-Smith and Kloess (2021) conducted a discursive psychology analysis of chat logs between one offender (posing as a teenage girl) and five victims under the age of sixteen in order to explore how children attempt to resist threats, and how offenders manage such resistance. The research identified an escalation in threats issued by the groomer following victims' resistance and non-compliance to requests. This study focussed on male victims, and the findings contradict studies that suggest that interactions with boys are less aggressive and forceful.

5.4 Children's Discourse in the Context of Groomers' Tactical Manipulation

Given space limitations, in the remainder of this section we select one aspect of children's discourse, namely how the child's use of language relates to groomers' manipulative tactics. Specifically, we examine the interactional behaviour of children by broadly 'chunking' their talk into agency-based categories that are linked to the groomer tactics. We label these categories as 'start', 'go' and 'stop'. 'Start' refers to when the child begins a sequence that is aligned to a groomer tactic – for example, if they were to volunteer a compliment, this would align to Praise (a sub-tactic of the DTD tactic; see Section 3); 'go' refers to when the child follows the groomer's lead; and 'stop' refers to when the child brings a sequence linked to a groomer tactic to an end.

'Start', 'go' and 'stop' represent different manifestations of child communicative agency. By selecting the intentionally neutral terms 'start', 'go' and 'stop', we attempt to avoid victim-blaming language, as might occur with alternative wording such as 'initiate' or 'continue'. In terms of the 'chunking' approach itself, we have deliberately simplified the interpretation of children's discourse for reasons of clarity of presentation: this is based on allocating chunks to the start-go-stop categories they most appropriately fit, while recognising that child–groomer interaction is a complex enmeshing of beginnings, middles and ends overlaying and intertwining with each other.

Figures 6 and 7 respectively show the percentage of use of start-go-stop instances in the children's and the groomers' discourse in the dataset.

While, as shown in Figure 6, in under a third of cases the children take on the role of introducing topics in their interactions with groomers, they primarily follow the groomer's lead (65 per cent) and infrequently (8 per cent) display 'stop' behaviours. With regards to the prominence of following the groomer's lead ('go'), it is important to note here the instances where the child indicates resistance, but this potential 'stop' does not succeed and is overcome by the groomer's manipulative facework. Such instances were coded as 'go' in our

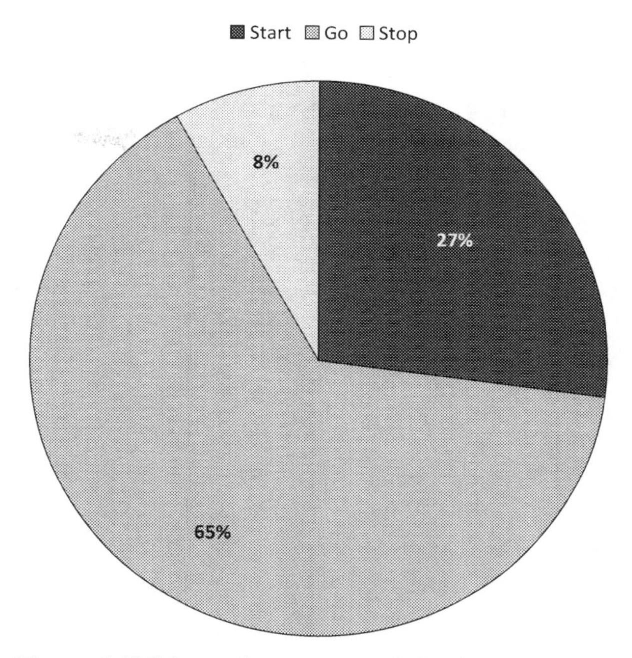

Figure 6 Child use of start-go-stop behaviours (per cent)

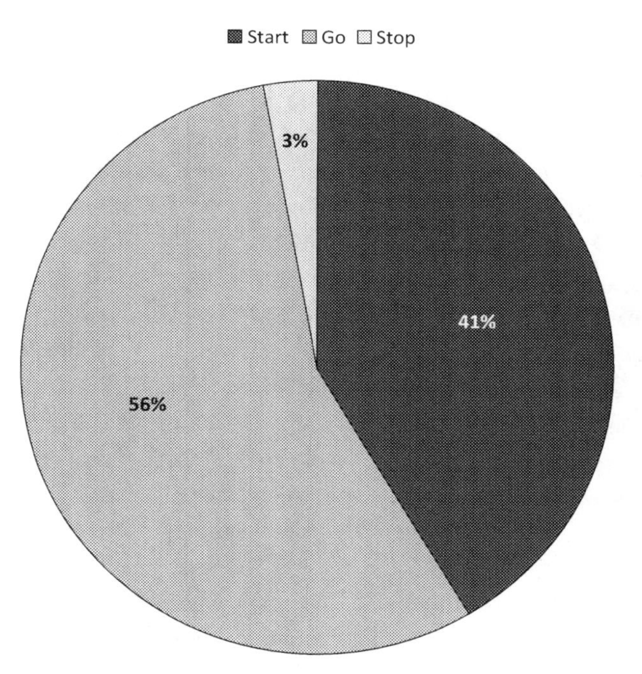

Figure 7 Groomer use of start-go-stop tactical behaviours (per cent)

analysis. In contrast, and as shown in Figure 7, the groomers introduce tactical behaviours much more frequently than children (41 per cent), suggesting their Directive role in driving the interactions (see Sections 3 and 4). Groomers primarily reflect and respond to children's behaviours, with most of their communication (56 per cent) classed as 'go'; that is, going along with the child. This indicates that they are sustaining the communication through their use of communicative tactics. Groomers 'stop' or halt the interaction half as frequently (3 per cent) as children. The distribution of start-go-stop instances varies across tactics (in the case of groomers) and children's alignment to those tactics, as discussed in Sections 5.4.1 to 5.4.3.

5.4.1 Start

Figure 8 presents the findings of our analysis of the category 'Start' in children's discourse, which show the percentage breakdown of instances of these in the children's discourse, as aligned to groomer tactics.

As Figure 8 shows, when children introduce topics in their interactions with groomers, these are most frequently aligned to the groomer SG sub-tactics of making explicit (16.85 per cent of children's 'starts') and implicit (13.14 per cent of children's 'starts') references to sex. The next most frequent alignment of children's 'starts' is to the groomer's DTD sub-tactic of Relationships (16.07 per cent of children's 'starts'). In the dataset, therefore, children are most frequently initiating discussion of topics regarding sex and relationships in the interactions with the groomer. This is perhaps not surprising because of the sexually focussed and relationship-building context of online grooming and may indicate children's pursuit of goals of sexual experimentation goals.

Next, we see that children's 'starts' are aligned to initiating interactions about the DTD sub-tactics of Activities (12.01 per cent of references), Sociability (14.7 per cent) and the Exchange of Personal Information (10.37 per cent), all of which occur in children's discourse with moderate frequency. Each of these elements of trust building are key to sustaining interactions – they are part of the social lubrication that lays the foundations for trust and relationship building. The evidence of children's initiation of these lines of discussion indicates a desire to build a friendship or connective relationship with the groomer. When it comes to discussions aligned to the groomer tactic of FC, children are observed to be introducing the topic of continued contact online more frequently (7.7 per cent) than broaching the possibility of meeting offline (4.75 per cent). Finally, children's 'starts' aligned to the groomer I tactic (both mental and physical) are barely present in our findings.

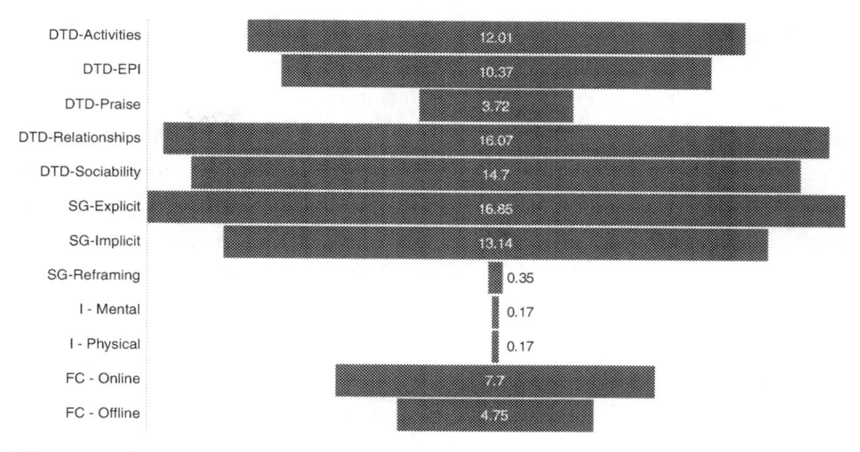

Figure 8 'Starts' in children's discourse aligned to groomers' tactics (per cent)

There may be multiple reasons for children's 'start' instances across the data, of which two seem most relevant. Firstly, starting interactions about these needs reflected groomer manipulation success which, as discussed in Section 2, relies on covertness regarding its abusive goal. Let's also recall in this regard Section 4.5, where we saw a typical example of how groomers encourage children to direct an exchange to give the child a false sense of being in control. Secondly, the children were seeking to pursue their own goals, based on their own wants, needs and wishes, which concerned sexual curiosity or experimentation, as well as deriving a sense of trust and reassurance about their forging a meaningful relationship with their interactions. This in turn relied on being able to maintain the interaction by, for example, seeking opportunities for continued communication, online or offline, with a grooming adult.

Example 5.2 illustrates how the child may start aspects of interactions with groomers in pursuit of their own interactional goals.

Example 5.2

01	Child:	Can we play that question game again that was funny xxx
02	Groomer:	Yes you start xxx
03	Child:	If I was older and we got into bed would you have gone all the
04		way with me xxx
05	Groomer:	Dunno xxx
06	Child:	Or are you a pussy
07		Xxx
08		Guess you're a pussy

The child's goal in Example 5.2 seems to be one of sexual experimentation and of testing boundaries as they ask the groomer to engage in a question-and-answer routine that they indicate they enjoyed previously ('Can we play that question game again that was funny', line 01). The child then asks the groomer how they would behave in a hypothetical sexualised scenario ('If I was older and we got into bed would you have gone all the way with me xxx', lines 03–04). When the groomer expresses coy uncertainty in their short response ('Dunno xxx', line 05), the child teases and goads them ('Or are you a pussy Xxx', lines 06–07; 'Guess you're a pussy', line 08) in a non-serious, bantering and flirtatious manner. Note, in this regard, the use of the x letter to represent kissing. This all suggests the child may also be experimenting with relationship roles, for example as the more confident/powerful party in their exchange with the groomer.

It is this type of 'start' that, when enveloped in narratives of 'risky behaviours' and 'active lifestyle choices', may lead to a blaming perspective by practitioners or the child themselves. The child's exploration of their experimental goals in this way also serves the groomer's purposes. This is because the topic of sex is forefronted conversationally, which may make the child feel confident and in control and, in turn, facilitate and mask the groomer's manipulation.

Example 5.3 illustrates how a child's 'starts' can be shaped by, and help advance, groomer manipulation:

Example 5.3

01	Child:	Can I see what you look like
02	Groomer:	I'm too shy at the moment
03	Child:	What do you mean to shy lol okay what ever you say
04		daddy
05	Groomer:	Like I need to trust you first and see how serious you are

In Example 5.3 the child is positioned as taking the lead in a conversation when the groomer presents as coy and cautious. The groomer manipulatively suggests they are the one at risk of being emotionally hurt, taking a 'vulnerability openness' stance (Lorenzo-Dus, 2023): 'I'm too shy at the moment' (line 02); 'Like I need to trust you first and see how serious you are' (line 05). Woven into the groomer's stance is a likely aim to deceive the child into believing that they are in control of the exchange. This serves to foster a sense of trust that may make children being groomed more susceptible and receptive to the manipulation to which they are being subjected.

5.4.2 Go

Figure 9 shows the percentage use of the category 'go', where children appear to follow the groomer's lead, as aligned to sub-tactic use.

As seen in Figure 9, there were three main ways in which children 'follow' groomers' tactical communication. Firstly, children seem receptive and respond most frequently to the groomer's DTD sub-tactic of Relationships (18.13 per cent), which once again points to relationship building and seeking as core interactional goals for the child. The next most frequent case where children 'follow' groomers' lead is in discussion of sex, in alignment with the groomer's SG sub-tactics. Figure 9 shows that children respond to and reciprocate the groomer's explicit SG (17.26 per cent) most frequently. They are also found to respond with implicit sexual terms (14.95 per cent), albeit slightly less frequently than explicit ones. Once again, children respond to the groomer's other DTD sub-tactics of Activities (10.39 per cent), Sociability (10.25 per cent) and EPI (9.81 per cent) with moderate frequency, which suggests their responsiveness to discussing topics to ease the communication and build a sense of mutual trust. Children respond to the DTD strategy of Praise (4.25 per cent) less frequently, which may indicate their doubt about the authenticity or appropriateness of the groomer's use of this strategy, especially given previous findings about the salience of compliments in groomers' discourse (Lorenzo-Dus and Izura, 2017).

A child may 'go along' with the groomer's use of tactics because this seems to align with and echo the child's own personal goals, as illustrated in Example 5.4.

Example 5.4

01	Groomer:	What's your favorite thing about yourself?
02	Child:	How open I am and that I don't judge
03	Groomer:	That's super cool. I really like that
04		How about physically?
05	Child:	My ass
06	Groomer:	Nice! Do you workout?

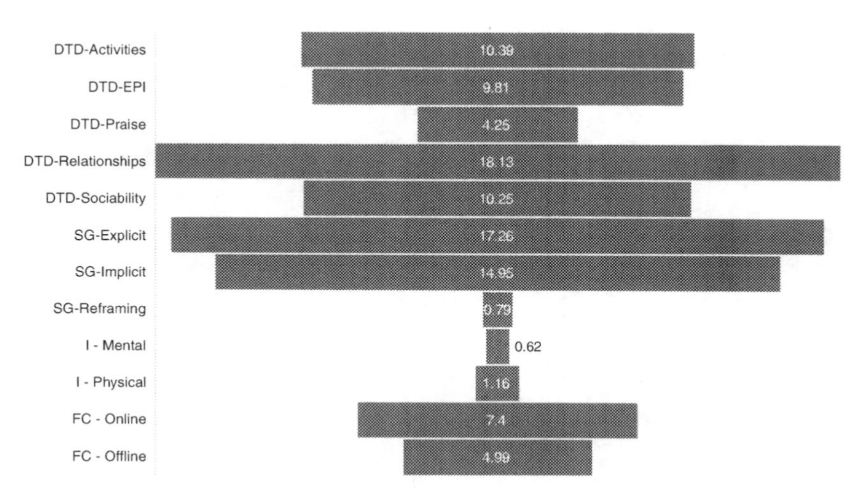

Figure 9 'Go's' in children's discourse aligned to groomers' tactics (per cent)

In this example, the child provides specific answers to getting-to-know-you-type questions from the groomer ('What's your favorite thing about yourself?', line 01). As discussed in Section 3, groomers regularly use Interrogatives within the DTD tactic. These sorts of personal questions manipulatively convey the impression that the groomer is interested in the child as an individual and that they may be looking to develop a personal relationship with them. This is also illustrated in Example 5.4 by the strongly encouraging feedback the groomer gives to the child's responses ('That's super cool. I really like that', line 03; 'Nice!', line 06). Developing a personal relationship is likely a communicative goal of the child in this example, as suggested by their considered and earnest response ('How open I am and that I don't judge', line 02) to the groomer's first question. With the groomer's relationship-building purposes seemingly aligned to their own, the child probably feels it is in their interests to go along with the groomer's questioning. Even when the groomer shifts the focus to the child's physical attributes ('How about physically?', line 04), in the context of the trust already established, their introduction of a slang term for a body part associated with sexual activity ('my ass', line 05) likely constitutes harmless flirtation within the child's testing of the bounds of the interaction.

A child may also 'follow' the groomer's lead out of curiosity or to try new experiences but without seemingly having a specific goal in mind, as illustrated in Example 5.5.

Example 5.5

01	Groomer:	Well entertain me please
02	Child:	Okay then I'll send you picks of me in my new dresses
03		and you can help pick the best one
04	Groomer:	Ooh ok
05	Child:	Would that help or not
06	Groomer:	Yea

In Example 5.5, the groomer uses a Directive speech act, expressed as a command, to get the child to display communicative behaviour that the groomer will find enjoyable ('Well entertain me please', line 01). The child agrees to the groomer's Directive ('Ok then I'll send you picks of me in my new dresses', line 02). As the groomer's goal is to engage the child in sexual activity, the word 'entertain' implicitly references something sexual. It constitutes an example of what is known to be groomers' frequent use of vague language to convey sexual intent (Lorenzo-Dus and Kinzel, 2021) that may provide them with cover should the child call them out on it or that may cast doubt in the child's mind when reflecting on their experience subsequently. The child in Example 5.5 undertakes to act on the groomer's command, offering to roleplay a fashion show ('I'll send you picks of me in my new dresses and you can help pick the best one', lines 02–03), placing the groomer in the role of judging their appearance. For the child, this exchange likely represents a goal of experimentation with flirting and attempting to test their control in the situation. The child only partially grants the groomer what they have asked for, creating a sense of bargaining on the part of the child ('would that help or not', line 06). This shows the child's agency in attempting to manage the groomer's demand for entertainment within the bounds of what, at that point, they are prepared to offer.

Children's communication also reflects the influence of the inherent power imbalance between child and adult groomer (see Section 4). Example 5.6 provides an illustration of this influence.

Example 5.6

01	Groomer:	Can I record it
02		Only I'll see it
03		Promise
04	Child:	Sure
05		Ye okay

In Example 5.6, the groomer exercises power over the child through their use of language. They do this by pressuring the child to agree to their Directive speech act, worded as a query preparatory ('Can I') request, to 'record' the conversation (line 01). After making the initial request, the groomer follows this up with a Commissive – an indirect speech act of promising to be discreet ('Only I'll see it', line 02), which is reinforced via a direct speech act of promising ('Promise', line 03) (see Section 3). All of this happens before the child has a chance to respond. The persistence in these repeated turns is not only indicative of groomers' fixated discourse, as seen also in Sections 3 and 4, but also of their stance of 'avidity'. This stance, as Lorenzo-Dus (2023) argues, is manipulatively oriented to the children being targeted for grooming. It creates a sense of expectation and force that likely influences the child's acceptance of the request. This is likely the case in Example 5.6, where the child follows up the groomer's first acceptance ('Sure', line 04) with a reworded and less definitive second ('Ye okay', line 05), the hesitancy suggesting that the child may have been rushed and coerced into a decision under pressure from the groomer.

5.4.3 Stop

'Stop' refers to children's communicative resistance to groomers' tactical manipulation. Child resistance with respect to groomer power abuse was examined in Section 4.5; in this section we examine it in relation to the start-go-stop chunking introduced earlier in this section. As seen in Figure 6, children sought to stop groomers. The percentage distribution of such attempts vis-à-vis groomer tactics is shown in Figure 10.

Figure 10 shows that the most frequent instances where children 'stop' their interactions with groomers are aligned to the groomer sub-tactics of SG-Explicit (29.23 per cent) and SG-Implicit (17.48 per cent). Children therefore end their conversations in almost half of the instances (46.71 per cent) of 'stops' in their discourse in response to the groomer's introduction of the SG tactic. This suggests that children are attuned and resistant to the inappropriateness of the groomer's sexualised communication. Children's stopping of groomers' discussion about relationships features next in frequency terms (15.47 per cent), followed by their resistance to groomers' attempts to extend or maintain their communication with the child online (11.75 per cent). This suggests that in some cases the groomer's discourse aligned to these tactics is perceived by the child to overstep the mark and warrant disengagement and a halt to the interaction. Less frequent in children's discourse are 'stops' related to groomer DTD sub-tactics (Praise, 5.34 per cent; Activities, 5.16 per cent; EPI, 3.62 per cent; Sociability, 3.41 per cent). This is not surprising as these sub-tactics are likely to appear 'benign'. The low frequency of 'stops' aligned to

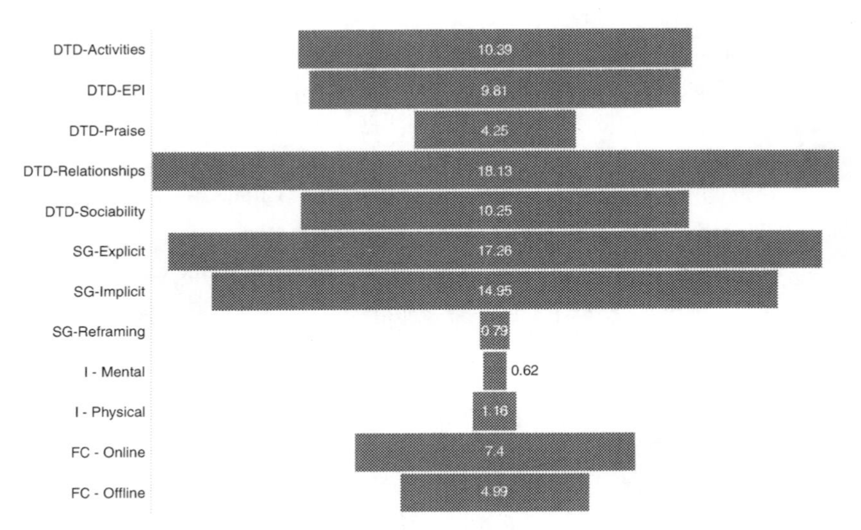

Figure 10 'Stops' in children's discourse aligned to groomers' tactics (per cent)

DTD sub-tactics suggests that children may be less attuned to trust-building tactics and therefore less alert to their relational function and impact, which in turn points to the need for a greater spotlight on interactions aligned to DTD to inform preventative approaches to counter OCSEA.

In the data, children's attempts at stopping particular groomer tactics can involve rejection, avoidance or delaying. An example of rejection was examined in Section 4 (Example 4.11) in the context of the analysis of children's communicative power. Here, we consider rejection in relation to the start-go-stop categorisation, examining the kind of interaction that can lead to a child's resistance to groomers' tactical work. This is illustrated in Example 5.7.

Example 5.7

01	Groomer:	we live too far anyway but you can still play along and have
02		fun;) lol
03	Child:	no you're alright
04	Groomer:	sudden change of moods? :/
05	Child:	no just not into that sort of thing
06		its a bit creepy
07	Groomer:	yeah I know :L not like i've asked you to fuck me :p sorry :/
08	Child:	ok bye
09	Groomer:	what the fuck LOL

The child in Example 5.7 deflects the groomer's attentions ('you can still play along and have fun', line 01) with a casual denial ('no you're alright', line 03). The groomer then challenges the child, flouting what is expected by changing their behaviour ('sudden change of moods?', line 04). The child resists further, clearly stating their position ('not into that sort of thing', line 05) and calling out the groomer for their behaviour, which they mark explicitly as inappropriate ('creepy', line 06), even if this is mitigated in terms of facework via the pre-modifying hedge 'a bit' (line 06). The riled groomer uses impoliteness: sarcasm ('yeah I know :L', line 07) and explicit disagreement that uses explicit sex talk ('not like i've asked you to fuck me', line 07). The latter also provides an opportunity to desensitise the child, albeit mitigated by a sticking out tongue emoji, which keys the content as a joke (':p', line 07) and an apology. This is, however, followed by an emoji indicating dissatisfaction ('sorry :/', line 07), which the child explicitly indicates their lack of concern about ('ok bye', line 08) – an example of the impoliteness strategy of snubbing, which succeeds at this point in bringing the conversation to an abrupt end. Here the child uses a digital affordance, namely the ability to terminate virtual contact and potentially block a user to reject the groomer's advance. The groomer's response ('what the fuck LOL', line 09) indicates incredulity at the child's bald rejection.

The groomer's reversion to humour, laughing and shrugging off the rejection may be an attempt on their part to save face following the child's explicit termination of contact.

A child will sometimes try to get out of, and therefore shield themselves from, certain conversational topics or actions, particularly those aligned to groomers' use of the SG tactic, as illustrated in Example 5.8.

Example 5.8

01	Groomer:	ooh 😉 haha :$ I'm not shy i'll show it straight off 😉 haha
02		(chuckle)
03	Child:	at the moment i just want a chat
04		Well
05		normally
06		😊 if that's ok?

In this example, the child responds to the groomer expressing their assurance and body/sexual confidence ('I'm not shy i'll show it straight off', line 01) by stating they want a non-sexual interaction ('at the moment i just want a chat', line 03). When revealing their willingness to expose themselves to the child, the groomer includes representations of laughter ('haha', line 01; '(chuckle)', line 02) and winky face emojis ('😉', line 01) to make sharing this information seem playful and naughty and thus aiming to include the child in collusion within the illicit game. This conflating of fun with sex is challenging for a child who may want to avoid sex talk but may be worried about threatening the groomer's face through non-reciprocation and/or losing face to the groomer by coming across like a killjoy or showing lack of maturity or experience. In Example 5.8, these considerations are reflected in the child's self- and groomer-oriented facework as part of their avoidance-communicative behaviour, namely the use of hedges ('Well / normally'; lines 04–05) and a smile emoji and confirmation tag ('😊 if that's ok?', line 06).

Another type of 'stopping' behaviour is when the child tries to avoid groomers' advances by delaying sexual engagement to a later date. This relational management on the part of the child is illustrated in Example 5.9.

Example 5.9

01	Groomer:	Ok then, but why agree to stuff to get me interested then
02		change your mind? Xxx
03	Child:	Because I am agreeing. Totally. Just not until I'm ready and
04		comfortable xxx

Here, delaying serves as a compromise between the child completely rejecting or completely 'going along' with the groomer's attempt to engage them in sexual activity (implicitly represented by the groomer's use of vague language 'stuff' (line 01)). In this example, the child's decision to delay sex rather than reject it entirely seems to be an attempt to appease the groomer's use of an accusatory, unpalatable question (an impoliteness strategy – see Culpeper, 2011) regarding the child's alleged prior agreement to sexual activity: 'why agree to stuff to get me interested then change your mind?' (lines 01–02). Despite the groomer's attempt to minimise the question's face-threat through positive politeness, namely the rendition of affection, specifically kisses ('xx', line 02), the groomer's annoyance is clear. This would be concerning for a child seeking to develop a meaningful personal relationship, particularly as children are socialised to please and defer to adults' wishes. The child's attempt to placate the groomer ('I am agreeing', line 03) is likely indicative of such concern. Delaying sex rather than ruling it out completely ('Just not until I'm ready', line 03) may feel like an acceptable way for the child to manage self- and groomer-oriented face needs, a way to keep the sexually motivated groomer interested as the child pursues their own friendship/romantic relationship goal. It could also represent an attempt to avoid the potential damage to face that could be caused by rejecting the groomer's advances explicitly. The child's assertion of the need to wait until 'I'm ready' (line 03) and 'comfortable' (line 04) is a brave assertion of boundaries of consent.

5.5 Conclusion

A focus on groomers, coupled with approaches to child behaviour that neglect an analysis of their actual discourse, means that children have to date been effectively silenced in research and practice seeking to combat online grooming. This situation runs counter both to our understandings about the interactional essence of grooming and to a child-rights and child-centred approach to safeguarding that recognises the child as a 'reflexive knowledge agent' (Beckett, 2019) with a right to be heard on issues that impact on them (UNCRC, Article 12).[24]

This section has sought to contribute to change this situation through its analytic focus on child discourse during online grooming. We have argued that this offers a yet unexplored means of building new research evidence about the shape of children's agency and the constraints acting upon it within a fundamentally abusive and exploitative online grooming context. Continuing to build this sort of research evidence, drawing on children's discourse, will help to ensure that practice and policy developments are as informed as possible by the realities of lived experience.

[24] www.unicef.org.uk/what-we-do/un-convention-child-rights/

Our analysis shows that children demonstrate the highest amount of agency when in the interactional position of either conversational leader ('start') or that of putting the brakes on a conversation ('stop'). Yet these are the communicative behaviours they are able to display least frequently, especially stopping groomers' tactical communication. Their agency is most constrained when in the role of conversational follower ('go'), which is the interactional position they display most frequently.

Our analysis also shows that children may 'go along' with groomers because to do so may appear to fit with their own goals: they may start elements of a conversation because groomers have persuaded them to roleplay a dominant part; their pushback may only avoid or delay rather than stop the advances of groomers; and so forth. What we are left with therefore is a complex picture that requires closer analysis to understand the intricacies of what works to bolster children's resistance, for whom and how, and to strengthen the support provided to children who have experienced and are recovering from online sexual abuse.

6 Conclusion: Applications of Research

6.1 Introduction

As stated in Section 1, our aim with this Element is to contribute new insights to knowledge about how language is used in online grooming in order to help combat the social problem that online grooming represents. While the first part of this aim is addressed by the research presented in the preceding three sections, a question that hangs over the second part is: will our findings actually make any difference? As with most academic studies, at the time of reporting, the 'real-world' impact of our research remains to be seen. However, the research presented throughout this volume is part of an applied research project – namely Project DRAGON-S, which we introduced in Section 1. A question that we do need to consider, as it concerns the raison d'être of the project, is: *can* our findings make a difference – specifically, is there a good prospect of the linguistics research presented in this Element helping to combat the criminal activity of online grooming and, thereby, improving the online safety of children?

This is the question that we address in this final section as we reflect on how our research can be applied to practice with reference to the project through which we are seeking to do this. More detail about Project DRAGON-S is thus provided in the next section (6.2.1), before discussing ways in which our research can have impact through this project in Section 6.2.2, and then ending the section (and Element) with some final remarks in Section 6.3.

6.2 Project DRAGON-S

6.2.1 Summary

Project DRAGON-S is an interdisciplinary project funded by the Safe Online Initiative at End Violence Against Children (EVAC).[25] It is the first applied research project globally to examine online grooming language use and, in doing so, to recognise the centrality of communication to online grooming. While linguistics methodologies are primarily used in the research underpinning Project DRAGON-S, these are synergised with approaches from other disciplines, including machine learning, criminology, psychology and public policy. The project was created to address the overwhelming volume and communicative sophistication of online groomers, and a gap in knowledge in child safeguarding and law enforcement agencies about how groomers and children communicate with each other online. For this purpose, two tools were developed in its initial phase (2021–2) and are being evaluated at the time of writing (2023): DRAGON-Spotter and DRAGON-Shield.

DRAGON-Spotter is a detection tool that has been created using a combination of linguistics and artificial intelligence methods. It generates a probability score based on how patterns in the language use of online conversations correspond to groomer communicative tactics, when applied to text where online grooming is suspected. DRAGON-Shield is a training portal that focusses on how online grooming works communicatively as part of two-way interaction between offenders and child-targets. This has been designed to help develop the knowledge and skills of practitioners involved in safeguarding children from OCSEA, such as social workers, educators, youth mental health workers, police officers and third sector workers.

The training content in DRAGON-Shield consists of three 'overview' modules and five 'tactics' modules that each explain an element of the model of online grooming discourse discussed in Section 3. While the primary focus of the training is on how groomers use language when engaging in tactical work to groom children, DRAGON-Shield also addresses how children use language (across the modules and in an overview module on child communication). The content of DRAGON-Shield is mostly built around real-life examples and contains mixed media features, including original animations, audiovisual excerpts of grooming interactions and interactive activities. To help practitioners test their knowledge, each module has a short quiz, and there is a final assessment at the end of the training. DRAGON-Shield also includes a chat simulator that allows practitioners to select response options in simulated interactions with a groomer, and to gain

[25] www.end-violence.org/safe-online

some insight of online grooming communication as a real-time conversational experience from the child's perspective. On completing the training and passing the final assessment, practitioners will gain access to a pack of resources and activities that can be used with the people they work with (e.g., colleagues, children, caregivers). This resource pack is based directly on the DRAGON-Shield training and has been designed to help practitioners to put their knowledge of online grooming as communication into practice.

6.2.2 Reflections on Applying Linguistics Research to Practice

In this section, we reflect on how findings from linguistics research can be applied to practice. We focus on the findings used in the development of DRAGON-Shield as these are directly linked to the research reported in this Element. With the linguistics knowledge that underpins the DRAGON-Shield content, our goal is to provide practitioners with insights and understanding about the role of language in online grooming so that this can support them in safeguarding children. We have sought to achieve this goal in a number of ways: by producing relevant, evidence-based training content that translates into knowledge that practitioners can apply in practice; by delivering this content in a format that is accessible and engaging; and by working closely with individuals and organisations, particularly child-safeguarding practitioners, children and lived-experience experts when developing and testing DRAGON-Shield.

Findings from the linguistics research that informs the DRAGON-Shield content includes those that illustrate the concept of language as action, as presented in Section 3. Such research-based content can support practitioners in understanding and explaining to others how sex talk in the context of online grooming is not *just talk*. This would help challenge perceptions of sexual chat being viewed as harmless fun, especially by children targeted by groomers. The kind of example that might be used to illustrate sex talk as abusive action is when groomers initiate – as part of an apparent bonding routine – an exchange of personal disclosures about past sexual experiences. This can be for the purpose of desensitising a child to sex talk while also gathering private information that the groomer could then use to manipulate the child into engaging in sexual activity with them.

A general finding across our research on the language of online grooming is that there are no signature words that serve as a smoking gun to indicate that grooming is taking place. Reasons for this include the fact that groomers often use language in a way that disguises their abusive intentions, such as when building trust (see Section 4.4), and because individual groomers can vary considerably in how they use language to manipulate children. However, this does not mean that there are no characteristic features in how groomers use language that transcend variation in style. One feature, noted in Sections 3 and 4, is the tendency for groomers to switch between using 'nice' and 'nasty' language; for example, when groomers mix impoliteness with positive and negative politeness strategies (see Section 4.3) to emotionally confuse child-targets when attempting to manipulate and control them. Knowledge such as this, provided through the DRAGON-Shield training, could help practitioners to better recognise when online grooming is taking place, and would also enable them to explain to children they work with how communicative manipulation works with reference to specific language examples.

An important aspect of the research used to create the content of DRAGON-Shield is that it focusses on the language of both groomers and children. Most previous research on online grooming communication has used data from the PJ corpus which, as noted in Section 2, consists of chat logs between groomers and decoys. By investigating how children use language in interactions with online groomers, we have produced findings that challenge false assumptions about the identity of victims of CSEA, for example that they are passive and helpless (see Section 5.2). As shown in Section 5, children can be active participants in interactions with groomers, including in sexual talk, which can reflect a child's experimentation or groomer's manipulation, but in no way diminishes the sense in which the child is a victim of abuse. The use of authentic examples in DRAGON-Shield can familiarise practitioners with the variety of ways that children use language in online grooming and reduce the risk of false ideas about how a victim should behave causing genuine victims to be overlooked.

Our research on children's use of language during online grooming has also highlighted the different ways that children resist groomers (see Sections 4 and 5). These suggest the potential for identifying strategies that children might use to deflect the advances of online groomers and to defend themselves against the harmful effects of their manipulation; for example, by using humour and sarcasm (see Section 4.6). Developing education around resistance strategies to grooming might help children who are emotionally embroiled in their connection with a groomer, particularly when they have been subjected to groomers' use of the DTD and Isolation tactics (see Section 3.3).

While there are many ways in which the linguistics research in DRAGON-Shield could improve the safeguarding of children against online grooming, this is entirely dependent on whether, and how much, the tool is adopted in practice. The inherent value of the research for advancing knowledge about online grooming discourse does not automatically translate into new knowledge for practitioners. It is for this reason that our research has an applied dimension and why we have created DRAGON-Shield. As noted in Section 6.2.1, this training portal includes a large number of examples, mixed media and interactive features that are designed to make the training engaging for practitioners. The content has been written in an accessible, non-academic style, and the inclusion of a downloadable pack of resources and activities provides a direct way for practitioners to put their training into practice.

To increase the likelihood of our research having a meaningful impact on practice and, through this, helping improve the online safety of children, Project DRAGON-S has included a programme of rigorous testing of DRAGON-Spotter and DRAGON-Shield, developing networks and partnerships with individuals and organisations who may use the tools, and collaborating with practitioners and individuals with lived experience of online grooming and other types of (O)CSEA. With DRAGON-Shield, the initial proof of concept underwent extensive consultation involving more than 180 child-safeguarding practitioners and 10 NSPCC service centres in England and Wales. During their development, both tools have undergone several stages of usability testing with intended end users. Overall, the two DRAGON-S tools have been co-produced in conversation with more than 250 individuals, including practitioners, researchers, lived-experience experts and children groups. This co-creation has allowed us to draw on the knowledge and expertise of people on the frontline of addressing the problem of online grooming. For example, practitioner perspectives on and knowledge about the different ways that certain kinds of language may be interpreted as victim blaming (see Section 5) have been vital for developing training content that is appropriate and reflects the values of practice. Ultimately, a key measure of success for an applied research project is how much it makes a real-world impact, and the primary means that we have used to achieve this with Project DRAGON-S are the collaborative relationships, including through iterative tool testing, piloting and evaluation, we have developed with people who share the common goal of combating online grooming and contributing to countering violence against children.

6.3 Final Remarks

Online grooming – how adults try and often succeed in manipulating children, how they develop and maintain abusive relationships, and how children respond to the actions of groomers – is fundamentally about communication, in particular the use of language. Yet, there has been a limited amount of linguistics research on online grooming. In this respect, the findings that have been presented in this Element represent an important contribution to an under-researched area. They also represent vital knowledge for practice that can be used in the development of detection tools and prevention resources to help combat online grooming. The applied research project that stems from this linguistics research, Project DRAGON-S, was designed for this purpose, and by working closely with practitioners to co-create DRAGON-Spotter and DRAGON-Shield, and rigorously and transparently evaluating both tools, we have modelled how research can deliver 'real-world' impact and help improve the safety of children online.

References

Addawood, A., Badawy, A., Lerman, K. & Ferrara, E. (2019). Linguistic cues to deception: Identifying political trolls on social media. *Proceedings of the 13th International Conference on Web and Social Media, ICWSM 2019* (June), Washington DC: Association for the Advancement of Artificial Intelligence (AAAI), 15–25.

Allan, K. (1997). Speech act theory: Overview. In P. Lamarque & R. Asher (Eds.), *Concise encyclopedia of philosophy of language* (pp. 454–66). Oxford: Pergamon.

Androutsopoulos, J. (2014). Languaging when contexts collapse: Audience design in social networking. *Discourse, Context & Media*, *4–5*, 62–73.

Austin, J. L. (1962). *How to do things with words*. Cambridge: Harvard University Press.

Bachenko, J., Fitzpatrick, E. & Schonwetter, M. (2008). Verification and implementation of language-based deception indicators in civil and criminal narratives. *Coling 2008 – 22nd International Conference on Computational Linguistics, Proceedings of the Conference*, *1* (August), Stroudsburg, PA: Association for Computational Linguistics, 41–8.

Baker, P. (2006). *Using corpora in discourse analysis*. London: Bloomsbury.

Bakir, V., Herring, E., Miller, D. & Robinson, P. (2019). Organized persuasive communication: A new conceptual framework for research on public relations, propaganda and promotional culture. *Critical Sociology*, *45*(3), 311–28.

Barendt, E. (2009). Incitement to, and glorification of, terrorism. In I. Hare & J. Weinstein (Eds.), *Extreme speech and democracy* (pp. 445–62). Oxford: Oxford University Press.

Beckett, H. (2019). Moving beyond discourses of agency, gain and blame: Reconceptualising young people's experiences of sexual exploitation. In J. Pearce (Ed.), *Child sexual exploitation: Why theory matters* (pp. 23–42). Bristol: Bristol University Press.

Benwell, B. & Stokoe, E. (2006). *Discourse and identity*. Edinburgh: Edinburgh University Press.

Blum-Kulka, S., House, J. & Kasper, G. (1989). Cross-cultural pragmatics: Requests and apologies. In S. Blum-Kulka, J. House & G. Kasper (Eds.), *The CCSARP coding manual: Cross-cultural pragmatics – Requests and apologies* (pp. 273–94). London: Ablex.

Bolander, B. & Locher, M. (2020). Beyond the online offline distinction: Entry points to digital discourse. *Discourse, Context & Media*, *3*, 4–26.

Brown, P. & Levinson, S. C. (1978/1987). *Politeness: Some universals in language usage*. Cambridge: Cambridge University Press.

Chiang, E. & Grant, T. (2017). Online grooming: Moves and strategies. *Language and Law / Linguagem e Direito*, *4*(1), 103–41.

Chiang, E. & Grant, T. (2019). Deceptive identity performance: Offender moves and multiple identities in online child abuse conversations. *Applied Linguistics*, *40*(4), 675–98.

Chibnall, S., Wallace, M., Leicht, C. & Lunghofer, L. (2006). *I-safe evaluation*. Final report. www.ojp.gov/library/publications/i-safe-evaluation-final-report

Christie, N. (1986). The ideal victim. In E. A. Fattah (Ed.), *From crime policy to victim policy*. London: Palgrave Macmillan.

Coupland, J. & Coupland, N. (2009). Attributing stance in discourses of body shape and weight loss. In A. Jaffe (Ed.), *Stance: Sociolinguistic perspectives* (pp. 227–49). Oxford: Oxford University Press.

Culpeper, J. (2011). *Impoliteness: Using language to cause offence*. Cambridge: Cambridge University Press.

Davidson, J., DeMarco, J., Bifulco, A., Bogaerts, S. & Caretti, V. (2016). *Enhancing police and industry practice*. EU Child Online Safety Project. London: Middlesex University.

Davidson, J., Martellozzo, E. & Lorenz, M. (2009). *Evaluation of CEOP ThinkUKnow internet safety programme and exploration of young people's internet safety knowledge*. London: Kingston University.

Davis, D. H. & Sinnreich, A. (2020). Beyond fact-checking: Lexical patterns as lie detectors in Donald Trump's tweets. *International Journal of Communication*, *14*, 5237–60.

de Fina, A., Schiffrin, D. & Bamberg, M. (2006). *Discourse and identity*. Cambridge: Cambridge University Press.

De Hart, D., Dwyer, G., Seto, M. C., et al. (2017). Internet sexual solicitation of children: A proposed typology of offenders based on their chats, e-mails, and social network posts. *Journal of Sexual Aggression*, *23*(1), 77–89.

Dodsworth, J. (2022). Child sexual exploitation, victim blaming or rescuing: Negotiating a feminist perspective on the way forward. In C. Cocker & T. Hafford-Letchield (Eds.), *Rethinking feminist theories for social work practice* (pp. 287–302). Cham: Springer International Publishing.

Egan, V., Hoskinson, J. & Shewan, D. (2011). Perverted justice: A content analysis of the language used by offenders detected attempting to solicit children for sex. *Antisocial Behavior: Causes, Correlations and Treatments*, *20*(3), 273–97.

Elliott, I. A. & Beech, A. R. (2009). Understanding online child pornography use: Applying sexual offense theory to internet offenders. *Aggression and Violent Behavior*, *14*(3), 180–93.

Ende, M. (1979). *The neverending story*. New York: Firebird.

Evans, C. & Lorenzo-Dus, N. (2022). Keywords in online grooming: A corpus-assisted discourse study. 10th International Symposium on Intercultural, Cognitive and Social Pragmatics (EPICS X), 23–25 May, Seville, Spain.

Finkelhor, D., Turner, H., Ormrod, R. & Hamby, S. L. (2009). Violence, abuse, and crime exposure in a national sample of children and youth. *Pediatrics*, *124*(5), 1411–23.

Gottschalk, P. (2011). A dark side of computing and information sciences: Characteristics of online groomers. *Journal of Emerging Trends in Computing and Information Sciences*, *2*(9), 447–55. www.cisjournal.org

Grant, T. & Macleod, N. (2016). Assuming identities online: Experimental linguistics applied to the policing of online paedophile activity. *Applied Linguistics*, *37*(1), 50–70.

Grant, T. & Macleod, N. (2020). *Language and online identities: The undercover policing of internet sexual crime*. Cambridge: Cambridge University Press.

Hallett, S. (2016). 'An uncomfortable comfortableness': 'Care', child protection and child sexual exploitation. *British Journal of Social Work*, *46*(7), 2137–52.

Hallett, S. (2017). *Making sense of child sexual exploitation: Exchange, abuse and young people*. London: Policy Press.

Halliday, M. (1978). *Language as social semiotic. The social interpretation of language and meaning*. London: Edward Arnold.

Halliday, M. (1994). *An introduction to functional grammar* (2nd edition). London: Edward Arnold.

Hamilton-Giachritsis, C., Hanson, E., Whittle, H. & Beech, A. (2017). Everyone deserves to be happy and safe. A mixed methods study exploring how online and offline child sexual abuse impact young people and how professionals respond to it. https://learning.nspcc.org.uk/research-resources/2017/impact-online-offline-child-sexual-abuse

Hamilton-Giachritsis, C. E., Hanson, E., Whittle, H. C., Alves-Costa, F. & Beech, A. R. (2020). Technology assisted child sexual abuse in the UK: Young people's views on the impact of online sexual abuse. *Children and Youth Services Review*, *119*, 1–10.

Hamilton-Giachritsis, C. E., Hanson, E., Whittle, H. C., et al. (2021). Technology assisted child sexual abuse: Professionals' perceptions of risk and impact on children and young people. *Child Abuse & Neglect*, *119*, 1–12.

Hanson, E. (2019). Understanding online forces and dynamics. In J. Pearce (Ed.), *Child sexual exploitation: Why theory matters* (pp. 87–116). Bristol: Bristol University Press.

Hanson, E. & Holmes, D. (2014). That difficult age: Developing a more effective response to risks in adolescence. Dartington: Research in Practice.

Hardie, A. (2012). CQPweb: Combining power, flexibility and usability in a corpus analysis tool. *International Journal of Corpus Linguistics*, *17*(3), 380–409.

Herring, S. C. (2013). Discourse in Web 2.0: Familiar, reconfigured, and emergent. *Discourse*, *2*(0), 1–26.

Holmes, J. (1995). *Women, men and politeness*. Harlow: Longman.

Hymes, D. (1974). *Foundations in sociolinguistics: An ethnographic approach*. Philadelphia: University of Pennsylvania Press.

Inches, G. & Crestani, F. (2012). Overview of the International Sexual Predator Identification Competition at PAN-2012. *Proceedings of the PAN 2012 Lab Uncovering Plagiarism, Authorship, and Social Software Misuse* (within CLEF 2012), 30.

Jakobson, R. (1960). Closing statements: Linguistics and poetics. In R. Innis (Ed.), *Semiotics: An introductory anthology* (pp. 145–75). Bloomington: Indiana University Press.

Jakobson, R. (1985). Poetry of grammar and grammar of poetry. In *Verbal art, verbal sign, verbal time* (pp. 37–46). Minneapolis: University of Minnesota Press.

Jay, A. (2014). *Independent inquiry into child sexual exploitation in Rotherham, 1997–2013*. Rotherham: Rotherham Metropolitan Borough Council.

Joleby, M., Landström, S., Lunde, C. & Jonsson, L. S. (2021). Experiences and psychological health among children exposed to online child sexual abuse: A mixed methods study of court verdicts. *Psychology, Crime and Law*, *27*(2), 159–81.

Jones, R. (2004). The problem of context in computer-mediated communication. In P. Levine & R. Scollon (Eds.), *Discourse and technology: Multimodal discourse analysis* (pp. 20–33). Washington, DC: Georgetown University Press.

Jones, R. (2012). *Discourse analysis*. London: Routledge.

Kidron, B., Evans, A., Afia, J., et al. (2018). *Disrupted childhood: The cost of persuasive design*. London: 5Rights.

Kloess, J. A., Hamilton-Giachritsis, C. E. & Beech, A. R. (2017). A descriptive account of victims' behaviour and responses in sexually exploitative interactions with offenders. *Psychology, Crime and Law*, *23*(7), 621–32.

Kontostathis, A., Edwards, L., Bayzick, J., Leatherman, A. & Moore, K. (2009). Comparison of rule-based to human analysis of chat logs. *Communication Theory*, *8*(2), 1–12.

Kopecký, K. (2017). Online blackmail of Czech children focused on so-called 'sextortion' (analysis of culprit and victim behaviors). *Telematics and Informatics*, *34*(1), 11–19.

Kopecký, K., Hejsek, L., Jana, K., Marešová, H. & Řeřichová, V. (2015). Specifics of children communication and online aggressors within the online assaults on children (analysis of selected utterances). SGEM 2015 International Multidisciplinary Scientific Conferences on Social Sciences and Arts, 195–202.

Kurzon, D. (1998). *Discourse of silence*. Amsterdam: John Benjamins Publishing.

Lalor, K. & McElvaney, R. (2010). Child sexual abuse, links to later sexual exploitation/high-risk sexual behavior, and prevention/treatment programs. *Trauma, Violence, & Abuse*, *11*(4), 159–77.

Lee, H.-E., Ermakova, T., Ververis, V. & Fabian, B. (2020). Detecting child sexual abuse material: A comprehensive survey. *Forensic Science International: Digital Investigation*, *34*, 301022.

Leech, G. N. (1983). *Principles of pragmatics*. London: Routledge.

Levinson, S. C. (1979). Activity types and language. *Linguistics*, *17*(5–6), 365–400.

Locher, M. A. & Watts, R. J. (2008). Relational work and impoliteness: Negotiating norms of linguistic behaviour. *Language Power and Social Process*, *21*, 77–100.

Lorenzo-Dus, N. (2021). 'It's the subtle language that gets to you': Understanding and managing researcher exposure to online child sexual grooming content. *8th annual BAAL Language and New Media SIG Event: Focus on the researcher – Dealing with distressing data*. York: British Association for Applied Linguistics.

Lorenzo-Dus, N. (2023). *Digital grooming: Discourses of manipulation and cyber-crime*. Oxford: Oxford University Press.

Lorenzo-Dus, N. & Kinzel, A. (2021). 'We'll watch TV and do other stuff': A corpus-assisted discourse study of vague language in child sexual grooming. In M. Fuster et al. (Eds.), *Exploring discourse and ideology through corpora* (pp. 189–211). New York: Peter Lang.

Lorenzo-Dus, N. & Izura, C. (2017). 'cause ur special': Understanding trust and complimenting behaviour in online grooming discourse. *Journal of Pragmatics*, *112*, 68–82.

Lorenzo-Dus, N., Izura, C. & Pérez-Tattam, R. R. (2016). Understanding grooming discourse in computer-mediated environments. *Discourse, Context and Media*, *12*, 40–50.

Lorenzo-Dus, N. & Kinzel, A. (2019). 'So is your mom as cute as you?': Examining patterns of language use by online sexual groomers. *Journal of Corpora and Discourse Studies*, *2*, 14–39.

Lorenzo-Dus, N., Kinzel, A. & di Cristofaro, M. (2020). The communicative modus operandi of online child sexual groomers: Recurring patterns in their language use. *Journal of Pragmatics*, *155*, 15–27.

Macdonald, S. & Lorenzo-Dus, N. (2021). Intentional and performative persuasion: The linguistic basis for criminalizing the (direct and indirect) encouragement of terrorism. *Criminal Law Forum, 31*(4), 473–512.

Martellozzo, E. (2013). *Online child sexual abuse: Grooming, policing and child protection in a multi-media world*. London: Routledge.

Melrose, M. (2010). What's love got to do with it: Theorising young people's involvement in prostitution. *Youth and Policy, 104*, 12–31.

Melrose, M. (2013a). Twenty-first century party people: Young people and sexual exploitation in the new millennium. *Child Abuse Review, 22*(3), 155–68.

Melrose, M. (2013b). Young people and sexual exploitation: A critical discourse analysis. In M. Melrose and J. Pearce (Eds.), *Critical perspectives on child sexual exploitation and related trafficking* (pp. 9–22). Basingstoke: Palgrave Macmillan.

Mikton, C. & Butchart, A. (2009). Child maltreatment prevention: A systematic review of reviews. *Bulletin of the World Health Organization, 87*(5), 353–61.

Milon-Flores, D. F. & Cordeiro, R. L. F. (2022). How to take advantage of behavioral features for the early detection of grooming in online conversations. *Knowledge-Based Systems, 240*, 108017.

Mishna, F., Cook, C., Saini, M., Wu, M. J. & MacFadden, R. (2011). Interventions to prevent and reduce cyber abuse of youth: A systematic review. *Research on Social Work Practice, 21*(1), 5–14.

Mullineux-Morgan, R. & Lorenzo-Dus, N. (2021). 'He says I have to do anything he says else he's coming to my house': A discourse impoliteness approach on children's perspectives on coercion in online child sexual grooming. 8th New Zealand Discourse Conference. 10–11 December, Christchurch, New Zealand.

Mullineux-Morgan, R. & Lorenzo-Dus, N. (2022). 'He supported me through so much, and he always listened'. 10th International Symposium on Intercultural, Cognitive and Social Pragmatics (EPICS X), 23–25 May, Seville, Spain.

Nettel, A. L. & Roque, G. (2012). Persuasive argumentation versus manipulation. *Argumentation, 26*(1), 55–69.

NSPCC. (2019). *Taming the wild web*. London: National Society for the Prevention of Cruelty to Children.

NSPCC. (2020). *How to win the wild west web*. London: National Society for the Prevention of Cruelty to Children.

NSPCC. (2021). *End-to-end encryption: Understanding the impacts for child safety online*. NSPCC report based on research undertaken by PA Consulting, April 2021. London: National Society for the Prevention of Cruelty to Children.

O'Connell, R. (2003). *A typology of child cybersexploitation and online grooming practices*. Preston: University of Central Lancashire.

Ofcom. (2022). Children and parents: Media use and attitudes report 2022. In *What children need* (March). https://doi.org/10.2307/j.ctv2d7x4jp.4

Ofsted. (2014). *The sexual exploitation of children: It couldn't happen here could it?* London: Ofsted.

Ofsted. (2016). *Time to listen: A joined up response to child sexual exploitation and missing children*. London: Ofsted.

O'Keefe, D. (2006). Persuasion. In O. Hargie (Ed.), *The handbook of communication skills* (pp. 333–52). London: Routledge.

Pardo, M. L. (2001). Linguistic persuasion as an essential political factor in current democracies: Critical analysis of the globalization discourse in Argentina at the turn and at the end of the century. *Discourse & Society, 12* (1), 91–118.

Partington, A. & Taylor, C. (2018). *The language of persuasion in politics: An introduction*. London: Routledge.

Pearce, J. (2009). Beyond child protection: Young people, social exclusion and sexual exploitation. In *Regulating sex for sale* (pp. 121–36). Cambridge: Policy Press.

Pearce, J. (2019). Bringing theory home: Thinking about child sexual exploration. In J. Pearce (Ed.) *Child sexual exploitation: Why theory matters* (pp. 1–22). Bristol: Bristol University Press.

Pendar, N. (2007). Toward spotting the pedophile: Telling victim from predator in text chats. International Conference on Semantic Computing (ICSC 2007), 235–41. www.computer.org/csdl/proceedings/icsc/2007/12OmNz2TCuG

Pennebaker, J. W., Boyd, R. L., Jordan, K. & Blackburn, K. (2015). *The development and psychometric properties of LIWC2015*. https://repositories.lib.utexas.edu/bitstream/handle/2152/31333/LIWC2015_LanguageManual.pdf

Powell, M. B., Casey, S. & Rouse, J. (2021). Online child sexual offenders' language use in real-time chats. *Trends and Issues in Crime and Criminal Justice, 643*, 1–15.

Quayle, E., Jonsson, L. & Lööf, L. (2012). *Online behaviour related to child sexual abuse*. childrenatrisk.eu. http://childrenatrisk.eu/robert_old/public/Interviews_with_affected_young_people.pdf

Reinharz, S. & Davidman, L. (1992). *Feminist methods in social research*. Oxford: Oxford University Press.

Reynold, E. & Ringrose, J. (2011). Schizoid subjectivities? Re-theorizing teen girls' sexual cultures in an era of 'sexualization'. *Journal of Sociology, 47*(4), 389–409.

Ringrose, J., Gill, R., Livingstone, S. & Harvey, L. (2012). *A qualitative study of children, young people and 'sexting'*. A report prepared for the NSPCC. London: NSPCC.

Schneevogt, D., Chiang, E. & Grant, T. (2018). Do Perverted Justice chat logs contain examples of overt persuasion and sexual extortion? A research note responding to Chiang and Grant (2017, 2018). *Language and Law/Linguagem e Direito*, *5*(1), 97–102.

Searle, J. R. (1969/1975). *Speech acts: An essay in the philosophy of language*. Cambridge: Cambridge University Press.

Searle, J. R. (1978). Intentionality and the use of language. *Studies in the Linguistic Sciences*, *8*(2), 149–62.

Seto, M. C. (2019). The motivation-facilitation model of sexual offending. *Sexual Abuse*, *31*(1), 3–24.

Seymour-Smith, S. & Kloess, J. A. (2021). A discursive analysis of compliance, resistance and escalation to threats in sexually exploitative interactions between offenders and male children. *British Journal of Social Psychology*, *60*(3), 988–1011.

Sidebotham, P. (2013). Culpability, vulnerability, agency and potential: Exploring our attitudes to victims and perpetrators of abuse. *Child Abuse Review*, *22*(3), 151–4.

Sorlin, S. (2017). The pragmatics of manipulation: Exploiting im/politeness theories. *Journal of Pragmatics*, *121*, 132–46.

Swales, J. (1990). *Genre analysis: English in academic and research settings*. Cambridge: Cambridge University Press.

Swales, J. (2004). *Research genres: Exploration and applications*. Cambridge: Cambridge University Press.

Taylor, J. (2020). *Why women are blamed for everything: Exposing the culture of victim-blaming*. New York: Little, Brown Publishers.

Terkourafi, M. (2011). From politeness1 to politeness2: Tracking norms of im/politeness across time and space. *Journal of Politeness Research: Language, Behaviour, Culture*, *7*(2), 159–85.

Topping, K. J. & Barron, I. G. (2009). School-based child sexual abuse prevention programs: A review of effectiveness. *Review of Educational Research*, *79*(1), 431–63.

UNICEF. (2020). *What works to prevent online and offline child sexual exploitation and abuse? Review of national education strategies in East Asia and the Pacific*. www.unicef.org/eap/

van Dijk, T. A. (2006). Discourse and manipulation. *Discourse and Society*, *17*(3), 359–83.

van Dijk, T. A. (2008). *Discourse and context: A sociocognitive approach*. Cambridge: Cambridge University Press.

van Dijk, T. A. (2017). How globo media manipulated the impeachment of Brazilian president Dilma Rousseff. *Discourse & Communication, 11*(2), 199–229.

van Gijn-Grosvenor, E. L. & Lamb, M. E. (2021). Online groomer typology scheme. *Psychology, Crime & Law, 27*(10), 973–87.

van Leeuwen, T. (1996). The representation of social actors. In C. Caldas-Coulthard and M. Coulthard (Eds.), *Texts and practices: Readings in critical discourse analysis* (pp. 32–70). London: Routledge.

Villacampa, C. & Gómez, M. J. (2017). Online child sexual grooming: Empirical findings on victimisation and perspectives on legal requirements. *International Review of Victimology, 23*(2), 105–21.

Walsh, K., Zwi, K., Woolfenden, S. & Shlonsky, A. (2018). School-based education programs for the prevention of child sexual abuse: A Cochrane systematic review and meta-analysis. *Research on Social Work Practice, 28*(1), 33–55.

Webster, S., Davidson, J., Bifulco, A., et al. (2012). European online grooming project: Final report. *European Commission Safer Internet Plus Programme, Tech. Rep.*, 1–152.

Whittle, H., Hamilton-Giachritsis, C. & Beech, A. (2014). 'Under his spell': Victims' perspectives of being groomed online. *Social Sciences, 3*(3), 404–26.

Whittle, H. C., Hamilton-Giachritsis, C. E., Beech, A. R. & Collings, G. (2013). A review of online grooming: Characteristics and concerns. *Aggression and Violent Behavior, 18*(1), 62–70.

WHO (2023). Adolescent Health. The World Health Organization. https://www.who.int/health-topics/adolescent-health#tab=tab_1

Widdowson, H. G. (2004). *Text, context, pretext: Critical issues in discourse analysis*. New York: Wiley.

Williams, R., Elliott, I. A. & Beech, A. R. (2013). Identifying sexual grooming themes used by internet sex offenders. *Deviant Behavior, 34*(2), 135–52.

Winters, G. M., Kaylor, L. E. & Jeglic, E. L. (2017). Sexual offenders contacting children online: An examination of transcripts of sexual grooming. *Journal of Sexual Aggression, 23*(1), 62–76.

Wolak, J. & Finkelhor, D. (2016). *Sextortion: Key findings from an online survey of 1,631 victims*. Janis Wolak & David Finkelhor CCRC in partnership with Thorn. www.unh.edu/ccrc/.

Woodby, L. L., Williams, B. R., Wittich, A. R. et al. (2011). Expanding the notion of research distress: The cumulative effects of coding. *Qualitative Health Research, 21*(6), 830–8.

Acknowledgement

Figure 1 was originally published in Digital Grooming: Discourses of Manipulation and Cyber-crime, by Nuria Lorenzo-Dus (2022) and is reproduced by permission of Oxford University Press.

Cambridge Elements

Forensic Linguistics

Tim Grant

Aston University

Tim Grant is Professor of Forensic Linguistics, Director of the Aston Institute for Forensic Linguistics and past president of the International Association of Forensic Linguists. His recent publications have focussed on online sexual abuse conversations including *Language and Online Identities: The Undercover Policing of Internet Sexual Crime* (with Nicci MacLeod, Cambridge, 2020).

Tim is one of the world's most experienced forensic linguistic practitioners and his case work has involved the analysis of abusive and threatening communications in many different contexts including investigations into sexual assault, stalking, murder and terrorism. He also makes regular media contributions including presenting police appeals such as for the BBC Crimewatch programme.

Tammy Gales

Hofstra University

Tammy Gales is an Associate Professor of Linguistics and the Director of Research at the Institute for Forensic Linguistics, Threat Assessment and Strategic Analysis at Hofstra University, New York. She has served on the Executive Committee for the International Association of Forensic Linguists (IAFL), is on the editorial board for the peer-reviewed journals *Applied Corpus Linguistics* and *Language and Law / Linguagem e Direito*, and is a member of the advisory board for the BYU Law and Corpus Linguistics group. Her research interests cross the boundaries of forensic linguistics and language and the law, with a primary focus on threatening communications. She has trained law enforcement agents from agencies across Canada and the US and has applied her work to both criminal and civil cases.

About the Series

Elements in Forensic Linguistics provides high-quality accessible writing, bringing cutting-edge forensic linguistics to students and researchers as well as to practitioners in law enforcement and law. Elements in the series range from descriptive linguistics work, documenting a full range of legal and forensic texts and contexts; empirical findings and methodological developments to enhance research, investigative advice, and evidence for courts; and explorations into the theoretical and ethical foundations of research and practice in forensic linguistics.

Cambridge Elements

Forensic Linguistics

Elements in the Series

The Idea of Progress in Forensic Authorship Analysis
Tim Grant

Forensic Linguistics in the Philippines: Origins, Developments, and Directions
Marilu Rañosa-Madrunio and Isabel Pefianco Martin

The Language of Fake News
Jack Grieve and Helena Woodfield

A Theory of Linguistic Individuality for Authorship Analysis
Andrea Nini

Forensic Linguistics in Australia: Origins, Progress and Prospects
Diana Eades, Helen Fraser and Georgina Heydon

Online Child Sexual Grooming Discourse
Nuria Lorenzo-Dus, Craig Evans and Ruth Mullineux-Morgan

A full series listing is available at: www.cambridge.org/EIFL